Wendy Boorer

Dogs

illustrated by David Nockels

Hamlyn · London

FOREWORD

This book was written to increase the pleasure and pride that dog-owners have in their pets, and to help would-be owners to choose a breed wisely. Over 130 breeds of dog are fully described and illustrated, and there are sections dealing with the origin of the dog, and the choice and care of both puppies and adults. Training the family pet is dealt with in some detail and the basic facts about breeding and rearing a litter are described. As well as discussing the dog in sickness and in health, the author includes a section on dogs at work, and illustrates the many uses to which man has put the dog's unique capabilities.

Published by The Hamlyn Publishing Group Limited
London · New York · Sydney · Toronto
Astronaut House, Feltham, Middlesex, England

Copyright © The Hamlyn Publishing Group Limited 1970
Reprinted 1972, 1974

ISBN 0 600 00082 6
Phototypeset by BAS Printers Limited, Wallop, Hampshire
Colour separations by Schwitter Limited, Zurich
Printed in Spain by Mateu Cromo, Madrid

CONTENTS

THE DOG AND MAN
Origin and history

The origins of the domestic dog are uncertain. Various theories have been advanced, none of which can be completely proved. The problem is the more complex as members of the genus *Canis*, of which the domestic dog is one, are closely allied to each other, and interbreed without difficulty. There is no doubt that the dog was the first animal to have been domesticated by Man and the earliest known domestication of dogs took place in south-western Asia, where the dog became his companion about 20,000 years ago. The dog was already domesticated by the time it reached northern Europe, at the latest by 6,000 B.C.

The possible ancestors of the dog include the jackal and the wolf. The jackal is a pack-hunting scavenger, common in all parts of the Middle East. It would have been a relatively easy animal for primitive Man to associate with. The jackal barks and howls, as a dog does, and hybrids between the jackal and the dog are fertile. However, the teeth of the jackal differ from those of the dog.

The wolf is also a pack-hunting animal, like the dog, and hybrids between wolf and dog are also fertile. The teeth of the wolf and the dog are the same. Though the wolf does not

Map showing the distribution of the wolf and jackal
(Pink) Wolf (Yellow) Jackal

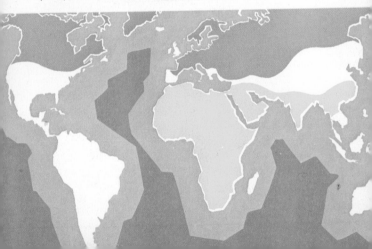

Wolf

Jackal

bark, barking appears to be a characteristic often acquired with domestication.

It is possible that the dog has more than one ancestor. Probably, tribes owning dogs of jackal ancestry moved northwards into lands where wolves lived, and crosses between dogs and wolves took place. At that time, wolves lived much further south than they do now.

The dog's first association with Man was probably as a scavenger, seeking food from the kills of primitive tribesmen. The constant presence of scavengers was useful to Man as a warning system of the approach of large carnivores. Later, men and dogs formed hunting packs, to the advantage of both. Possibly men reared puppies in their camps to form a source of food when times were hard. Later, but still quite early on in the process of domestication, men used dogs to herd and protect sheep and goats. This was a logical development of the tendency common to both wolves and jackals. Both drive herds of their prey while waiting for the right moment to single out a victim from the mass. By the time the dog reached Europe, it was probably already a sheepdog.

Domestication

While we do not know when or where the dog became domesticated, we do know some of the effects of this process. One important effect is that a domesticated animal is much less fearful of Man. Besides this profound psychological change in the dog, the animal becomes subject to variations in colour, and the proportions of its body and the skull change. The skull changes affect the brain case, the teeth, and the bones of the ear. The animal's skin retains juvenile folds and dewlaps in adult life. The length of the digestive tract increases. Abnormal tails, shortened legs, and flattened muzzles all appear, and successive generations of domestic animals tend to retain these characteristics.

Among primitive dogs still existing, which possibly represent steps along the way to domestication, is the Australian Dingo. The Dingo was a domesticated animal when it migrated

Dingo

with Man to Australia in the Middle Stone Age. Once there, it reverted to the wild. Being alert, wary, and intelligent, it is remarkably successful in doing a great deal of damage to sheep as well as smaller game. The average height of the Dingo is about twenty inches, and its colour varies from reddish to pale fawn.

The Dingo is a kind of animal somewhere between the

ancestral dog types and the Pariah or Pi dog. Pariahs are the ownerless street dogs found from the Balkan Peninsula to Australia, from northern Africa to Japan. They differ in type from place to place, some resembling the Sheepdog, some the Dingo, some the primitive Greyhound. Though men have made a number of special studies of Pariahs, they have been unable to decide whether Pariahs are wild descendants of earlier domesticated breeds, or dogs in the first stages of domestication.

Still closer to domestication are a number of African hunting dogs, about which little is known. One of these, the Basenji, has recently been established in Britain and the United States. It retains two characteristics of wild dogs. Firstly, the bitches only come into season once a year, against twice a year for more domisticated breeds. Secondly, Basenjis do not bark. Salukis can also claim an unbroken ancestry to the earliest days of human civilization, for they are very similar to some long-haired Greyhounds prized by the Ancient Egyptians.

Typical Pariah dogs

Great German Spitz

Classification

The classification of the domestic breeds of dog has occupied various canine authorities since the time of the Romans. No classification has been devised which included all the known distinct breeds. But some types in the family of dogs are so markedly similar that it is worth listing them.

Spitz group

One of the basic families of breeds is the Spitz group, which has a broad skull, with a pointed muzzle. They carry their tails curled over their backs, and their ears are erect and pointed. These characteristics can be recognized in animals as far apart geographically as the Siberian Husky and the Japanese Akita.

Sheepdog group

The second group consists of the Sheepdog family, which shows a good deal of variation. They are possessive, intelligent dogs, with weather-resisting coats. They have a characteristic slinking gait which enables them to cover a lot of ground economically. The Alsatian is typical of this group of dogs.

Groenendael, member of
the sheepdog group

Sloughi, member of the
greyhound group

Greyhound group

The third group, and one of the most ancient, is the Greyhound family. These dogs are built for speed, and they hunt
by sight rather than by scent, without giving tongue. From
the Deerhound to the Italian Greyhound, they all possess the
long legs and lean outline of a running animal.

Hound group

The Hound group proper consists of dogs that follow their quarry by scent and give tongue. The Hounds, with their long, pendent ears and domed skulls, developed from the Greyhounds, and the Spaniel-Pointer-Setter group are descendants of the Hounds. They possess the long ears and good noses of Hounds, allied to a more biddable temperament.

Mastiff group

A group whose origin is uncertain is that of the Mastiff-like dogs. Nearly all the big dogs belong in this group, together with those with flattened muzzles, such as the Boxer and the Bulldog. The Romans found large dogs of this kind when they invaded Britain, and exported them to fight in the Roman arenas.

Dogue de Bordeaux, member of the mastiff group

Terrier group

The last group consists of the Terriers. Many of these animals are wiry-coated, small to medium sized dogs, with courageous, excitable temperaments. Strong for their size, hardy, and often quarrelsome, Terriers are the extroverts of dogs.

OWNING A DOG

Choosing a dog is almost too easy. All puppies are appealing, and it is very easy to give one a home without clearly visualizing the consequences. As a result, thousands of dogs are abandoned every year. All would-be dog owners should ask themselves the following questions before taking a dog into the home: Is someone at home most of the day? No dog should be left alone while all the family go out to work. Is someone prepared, and responsible enough, to exercise the animal every day? In the era of the motor-car, the days are past when it was possible to turn a dog out for exercise. Can you afford to feed the type of dog that you want? For example, in Britain, at present-day prices, a dog the size of an Alsatian will cost something like £125 a year to feed. Are

German Hunt Terrier

you prepared to pay for the inoculations that will protect your puppy against distemper? The inoculations vary in price. In Britain an average veterinary fee would be around £6. Lastly, are you prepared to book boarding accommodation for your dog when you book your own holiday? Far more pets are jettisoned at holiday time than at any other.

If you have considered all these points and still want to be a dog owner, the following considerations may help in the choice of a pet. Do you want an adult or a puppy? An adult dog will already be set in its ways and may well have habits, such as incessant barking or chasing cats, which you do not like and will find difficult to change. Having already been passed on from one owner to another, it will be less likely to give you its complete devotion. However, you will be saved the mess and the drama of bringing up a puppy,

and you may well feel like giving a home to one of the strays that would otherwise be destroyed. If you do get one from the animal charities, you can at least be sure that it is healthy.

You must also decide whether to have a mongrel or a pedigree animal. The mongrel puppy can grow up to any size and shape, whereas with a pedigree puppy you know what the result will be. Mongrels are not more intelligent or healthier than pedigree dogs. The cost of feeding and caring for either is the same so, if owning a pedigree animal gives you pleasure, the initial cost of a pedigree puppy is a small price to pay over the years of ownership.

You can also choose whether to have a dog (male) or a bitch (female). A bitch will *come into season* twice a year, for six weeks altogether. During this time she will be attractive to dogs, and may mate, given the opportunity. Bitches are more affectionate and less inclined to roam.

If you decide to have a pedigree animal, the number of breeds presents a bewildering choice. The best place to see them all is at a championship show. These are held in many places during the year. Dates and locations are published in the various dog magazines. Consider the size of dog you can cope with, and also the amount of time you can spend on grooming. There is a standard description of an ideal speci-men of each breed, which may be obtained from your kennel club or other canine organization for a small fee.

The descriptions of the various breeds on pages 86–155 include maximum heights and weights as a basis for compari-

Adult or puppy, these are both Rough Collies.

son. It should be remembered that dogs are slightly larger than bitches. Something of the breed history is also included, because it can give some clue to a dog's temperament. There tend to be fashions in breeds. If you are not bent on following the fashion, you might consider some of the breeds whose numbers are very small. They are often kept in being by a handful of devoted breeders.

Your first puppy
Choosing a puppy
A healthy puppy is fat but not unduly pot-bellied, and has a loose, supple skin and clear, bright eyes. Avoid any dog with a discharge from the eyes or nose. If you are choosing from a litter, check that the surroundings are clean and vermin-free. Look carefully at the mother. A bitch that has just reared a litter often looks unkempt, but should not appear half-starved. Pedigree pups are usually offered for sale at eight weeks, and this is a good age to buy. Puppies younger than this can still be reared, but they need extra care. Choose the boldest, liveliest puppy, not the one that

hangs back or hides in corners. The same rules apply if you choose in a pet shop or dealer's. If any of the puppies in a shop looks ill, do not buy there, as the odds are that all the puppies are infected.

Finding a puppy

If you have decided on a particular breed of dog, you can look in the dog magazines, which list puppies for sale under breed headings each week. Alternatively, your kennel club will give you the name and address of the secretary of the breed club, who should be able to tell you of the nearest kennel. The price for a pet puppy varies from breed to breed. In Britain, it should be somewhere between £15 and £50. With the puppy you should get a completed pedigree form, and either a registration certificate (if the puppy has already been registered) or a registration form, signed by the breeder, if the registration is being left to you. The breeder should also tell you when the puppy was last wormed, and if it has been inoculated. Some breeders also give diet sheets which give details of their feeding.

Try to avoid the shy puppy which does not want to make friends.

Worming and inoculation

Nearly all puppies have round worms. A responsible breeder will worm puppies before they are sold at eight weeks, and it is wise to worm them again at four months. There are reliable proprietary brands of worm pills, but as the drug used is a powerful one the instructions should be followed carefully. All puppies should be protected by inoculation against hardpad, distemper, canine virus hepatitis, and two leptospiral infections. This list is not quite so formidable as it sounds, as the vaccines are combined. But the diseases are all killers, and until your puppy is protected it should not be allowed near any other dog. A veterinary surgeon will advise you as to the best time for inoculation against these diseases (it is usually at twelve weeks), and also when booster doses are necessary.

A puppy at eight weeks is still a baby, and like all babies it needs warmth, plenty of rest, small, frequent meals, and lots of affection. A young puppy needs at least four meals a day. The size of the meals should be increased and the number cut down progressively: three meals a day at three months; two meals a day at six months; one meal a day at a

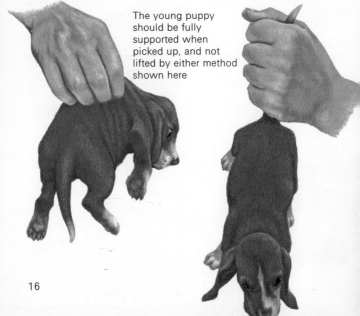

The young puppy should be fully supported when picked up, and not lifted by either method shown here

Make the puppy feel safe and secure

year. Start the puppy off with two meat meals a day. The meat can be either raw or cooked, and should be cut to a size that the puppy can manage. You should also give two milk meals with cereal or puppy meal added. Add a few drops of cod-liver oil to one of the daily meals. A rough guide to the amount of food to give a puppy is how much the animal will eat in ten minutes, after that it will probably lose interest.

Holding a puppy

A puppy should always be picked up so that the whole of its body is supported. A firm but gentle hold is necessary because puppies wriggle, and a fall from someone's arms can be a serious matter for a young pup. A bitch picks her puppies up by the scruff (nape) of the neck, but by eight weeks they are already too big and heavy for this to be a comfortable way of carrying them. A firm hold under the belly will give the puppy the reassurance it needs.

Sleeping quarters
Dog beds
Every dog should have a draught-proof bed of its own. Because many puppies chew anything within reach, a cardboard box turned on its side makes as good a bed as any. The box can easily be replaced as the pup grows. Wicker dog baskets are not good things to buy, as many dogs find them irresistible chewing material. More important, such baskets are difficult to keep clean, provide a splendid hiding place for fleas, and do not keep out draughts. You can buy a dog bed consisting of a metal frame with canvas sides and bottom. Beds of this kind are made in sizes to fit all breeds,

A dog box, and a good example of a dog bed

and have the great advantage that the canvas can easily be taken off and washed. A bed for an adult dog can be made from tongued and grooved boarding. It should consist of a platform an inch or two from the ground, big enough for the animal to lie down flat, and sides a few inches high.

Puppy pens
A collapsible puppy pen is sometimes a good thing to buy, because a puppy can then be left with absolute safety. Some terriers and toy dogs go to shows in their own dog boxes, and such boxes are very useful, particularly if you plan to travel with your dog a lot. A puppy can be accustomed to the box by being shut in it for a few minutes with a titbit.

The first night
Every puppy brought away from the litter will protest when it first finds itself alone, and it usually howls for the first few nights. If you do not want the dog to sleep in your bedroom, you must be firm. The puppy should be left in its bed with a well-wrapped, hot-water bottle. Usually a day full of excitements will have tired it, so that the expected howls do not begin until the small hours. By all means comfort the animal; a few words and a warm drink may let everyone go back to sleep. Most puppies soon give up making a noise, but they often turn their energies to chewing instead, which is why puppy pens are a good investment. Chewing is a necessity until their adult teeth come through at four to five months. Pet shops sell a variety of toys for dogs. Choose the indestructible ones, or those made of cowhide.

Choose really tough toys

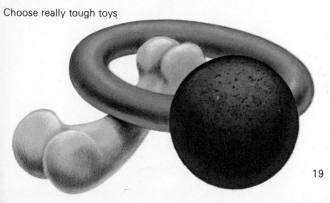

Cleanliness and diet

House training

House training is not such a difficult business as is often suggested. It does, however, take time and patience. At eight weeks a puppy has little control over its bowels and bladder, but it has an instinct to keep its bed clean and will leave its box before relieving itself. Once it has soiled a spot, the smell there will tend to trigger off further puddles every time the puppy passes. For this reason, every mistake in the house should be cleaned up with a disinfectant strong enough to hide the original odour from the dog. A puppy should be taken out at least every two hours at first, and praised lavishly when it relieves itself outside. A puppy wants to go out immediately after every meal, as soon as it wakes from a sleep, and after any energetic play. Few puppies can be expected to be dry at night before they are six months old, though they may be clean in the daytime before this age.

Planning the diet

Because a dog is a *carnivore* (meat-eater) and a scavenger,

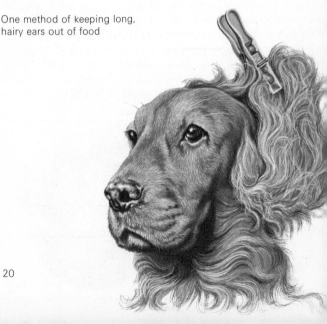

One method of keeping long, hairy ears out of food

meat – and sometimes very smelly meat – would be its main food in wild life. When wild animals have made a kill they usually eat the paunch of their victim first. The partially digested vegetable matter in the stomach provides vitamins and trace elements which would otherwise be absent from an all-meat diet. This must be remembered in planning your dog's diet. Meat should form at least two-thirds of the diet. There is really no need to cook it or to cut it up. If you prefer to cook it, the cooking should not be prolonged. The liquid in which the meat was cooked should also be fed to the dog, as it contains some of the minerals in the food. Food should not be minced or ground and left open to the air for long periods, because this destroys the vitamin content. Always take the chill off food that has been kept in a refrigerator. The idea that a dog should not have fat is a mistaken one. Provided that the proportion is kept to a reasonable level, fat is beneficial. Offal is very good, but should not be given more than once a week. The same rule applies to fish. Fish-bones should never be fed to dogs, but it is possible to pressure-cook whole fish (about thirty minutes at fifteen pounds pressure) so that the bones crumble and the whole lot is edible.

Raise the dish for a very large dog

Do not feed at the table

Canned dog foods are extremely convenient, but they are an expensive way of feeding. In some countries, the law does not require the constituents of a pet food to be printed on the label, so you cannot be sure exactly what you are getting.

Biscuits and bones
If two-thirds of the diet is meat or fish, the rest can be made up of scraps or the largest dog biscuits that your dog is prepared to tackle. Biscuit meals served soggy with gravy are bad for the teeth. Large raw marrow bones often give a dog a lot of enjoyment, but smaller cooked bones should not be given. Cod-liver oil should be added to the diet of puppies, expectant and nursing bitches, and old dogs. Another useful supplement is yeast tablets, which provide the B complex of vitamins. All dogs seem to enjoy them.

Size of meals

The amount of food needed by each dog varies. A very rough guide is the amount your dog will eat in ten minutes, or alternatively two-thirds of an ounce of food per pound of the dog's body weight each day. A working dog may need up to four times this amount. Growing puppies and expectant and nursing bitches obviously need more food, too.

Exercise

Many pet dogs could do with more exercise than they get. A daily walk of three to four miles, part of it off the lead, should be a must for all except toy dogs. The larger the dog and the more racily built it is, the more exercise it needs. Provided it is adequately fed and worked up to the exercise gradually, no healthy dog can have too much walking.

All dogs need free galloping

Hound glove

Thinning scissors

Grooming and care

Grooming

Grooming should be carried out daily. Brush smooth-haired breeds with a special glove called a *hound glove*, and polish their coats with a duster. With long-haired breeds daily attention is essential, though ten minutes' brushing and combing are all that is required. Hair is most likely to become matted behind the ears, between the toes and inside the thighs. If a mat of hair cannot be teased out, cut it away.

Trimming

If your dog is of a breed that requires trimming or clipping, you can either have it done professionally at regular intervals, or learn to do it yourself. A demonstration by an expert will teach you a great deal. A photograph of a well-trimmed show specimen is also a good guide. If you are merely trimming a pet terrier, you can use a special *stripping knife* to take off the old coat. If you are preparing the dog for showing, the slower method of plucking out the hair between the finger and thumb gives a better finish.

Daily care of the coat

enables you to spot fleas quickly. All dogs get fleas, from time to time. Use a flea powder recommended for dogs. In summer, grass seeds can cause a lot of trouble to a long-haired dog.

Bathing

Dogs should be bathed as little as possible. Newspaper is very useful when drying dogs that are wet and muddy. Mud is easily brushed off when the animal is dry. There are proprietary brands of dry-cleaning powder which can be rubbed into the coat and then brushed out. This dry-cleaning method is particularly useful with old dogs or young puppies which must not be bathed. If a bath becomes essential, the water should be lukewarm and quite shallow. Lift the dog in gently and wet it with water from a jug, leaving the head dry. Work up a good lather with a shampoo, using either the kind for dogs or the kind for humans. Never use detergent or washing soap. Rinse well. Finally, wash the dog's head, being careful not to allow water to get into its ears. Drying can be accelerated by use of a hair dryer, and it should not go out until dry.

A brush that fits the hand comfortably

Choose a comb with blunt teeth

Teeth and ears

Most dogs have good teeth if they are not fed too much sloppy food. Marrow bones, large, hard biscuits, and lumps of raw meat all help to keep the teeth clean. A veterinary surgeon will descale teeth that are heavily covered with tartar. He may recommend cleaning the teeth daily with a soft toothbrush.

The insides of the ear-flaps need occasional cleaning with cotton-wool. Most dogs do not object, provided the cleaning is done gently. Wrap cotton-wool around a match-stick and soak it in olive oil. Never poke anything down the ear canal itself. Water in the ears can set up infections, so always plug a dog's ears with cotton-wool when bathing it. Dogs with pendent ears or hair-filled ear canals are liable to ear troubles, all of which are very painful to the animal. If your dog shakes its head a lot and its ears smell offensive, take it to a vet.

Cutting nails

Most dogs whose nails are long would benefit by more road walking exercise. Toy dogs and old dogs may need their nails cut if they have grown long enough to make walking uncomfortable. Special clippers must be used, as scissors are useless. The nail has a living quick growing down inside it, and if this is cut it is extremely painful to the dog. In white

Types of ear: *from left to right*, prick, button, semi-prick pendent, rose, bat

nails, the blood line of the quick can be seen and avoided. But dark nails give no indication where the quick is, so only a small amount of nail should be taken off at a time. Many dogs object to the whole process strenuously, and you may find it easier to file the nails with a fine metal-worker's file for five minutes a day. Dew-claws in all breeds should be checked regularly, as they can grow round in a circle.

The old dog
Care of an old dog is largely a matter of common-sense. It should not be allowed to become wet or chilled. Allowances should be made for the fact that its hearing, sight, and teeth might not be as good as they were. It should also be protected from boisterous children and puppies.

The dew-claw is found on the inside of the leg above the foot.

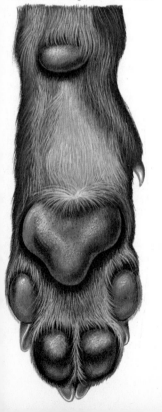

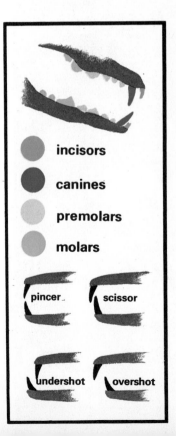

incisors

canines

premolars

molars

pincer

scissor

undershot

overshot

Your dog's life could depend on the quality of these collars and leads

Training
Collars and leads

Puppies up to the age of six months do not need exercising, as such, but they should be taken out to help them to become accustomed to noise and traffic. A puppy should be introduced to its collar and lead as soon as it has been inoculated and can go out. Puppy collars and leads need only be light in weight, but the collar must fit tightly enough to prevent the puppy pulling it over its head in moments of panic. Adult collars and leads should be of good quality. In an emergency your dog's life could depend on the lead holding under strain. The catch on the end of the lead is often the weakest link. Try to get one where the opening is not at the point of the greatest strain. A flat, wide collar is suitable for smooth-coated dogs, but a rolled one will mark the neck of a long-coated dog less. To preserve the neck frill on long-coated breeds, the dogs should only wear collars when actually going out. A choke chain gives a greater degree of control than a leather collar. It must be correctly put on and correctly used. The chain

Slip chain used in training

links are slipped through one of the end rings to form a loop. With the dog on the left-hand side, the loop should be put over its head, in such a way that the sliding ring is attached to the end of the chain which is coming under the dog's neck. The lead is then clipped to the free ring. If the collar is put on the correct way round it will tighten when the lead is pulled and loosen automatically when the lead is slack.

The first walks

When first taking a puppy out on a collar and lead, you need time for patient coaxing. A puppy that appears terrified should wear its collar and lead in the house until it is completely used to them. If a puppy sits down and nothing will budge it, you will have to pull it gently until it realizes that walking is an easier method of progression. An adult dog that has developed the bad habit of hauling its owner after it can be cured with patience and the use of a choke chain. As soon as the dog pulls, the lead should be jerked hard. Never let the dog lean on the collar, but always jerk it back as soon as it pulls, and it is surprising how quickly an animal will learn that pulling will pinch its neck uncomfortably.

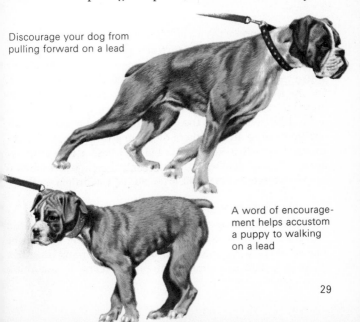

Discourage your dog from pulling forward on a lead

A word of encouragement helps accustom a puppy to walking on a lead

29

Gutter training

It is very important, too, to teach puppies not to soil the footpaths. As soon as your dog begins to squat it should be pulled quickly to the gutter, and praised when it gets there. For the first few times, it will probably be too surprised to do anything at all, but most puppies learn quite quickly to make their own way to the gutter. It is indefensible to allow one's animal to annoy others by fouling the footpaths. Some young dogs when unduly excited will pass a few drops of urine. This, of course, is an involuntary action and should not be corrected. They will grow out of it with maturity.

Checking bad habits

One of the advantages of having a puppy is that you can prevent bad habits forming. Though dogs of any age can be trained, it is always much easier to teach something new than to break a bad habit formed over the years. If you think

Dogs that are allowed to roam can get into trouble

ahead to the behaviour you would like from your adult dog, you will not allow your puppy to jump up and lick your face, or chase after the postman with loud barks.

The first thing that any puppy should learn is the meaning of the word 'No'. This in effect means 'Leave it alone', so unless you are in a position to see that your puppy does leave it alone, do not say 'No'. When you give a command to a puppy which you cannot enforce, and the dog disobeys, you are merely teaching it to ignore your voice. Prohibitory commands like 'No' should always be growled in a harsh tone. When calling a dog to you, always use a pleasant tone.

Chasing cats and other domestic animals must be firmly discouraged. All dogs will chase anything that runs, and once they are chasing are practically impossible to stop in mid-flight. To discourage chasing, lead your puppy into temptation as much as possible and shout 'No' as soon as it begins to display any interest.

Nervous puppies

Nervous puppies are difficult to deal with, as they need much kindness and time. If possible, it is best to avoid owning one. But some owners make their dogs nervous. Whenever a puppy has a strange and frightening experience, it should be encouraged to overcome its fear by being spoken to in calm and confident tones. Too much sympathy will lead the animal to suspect that its fears are not entirely groundless. In particular, this applies to meeting other dogs. No dog, even a confirmed fighter, will attack a puppy, so it is quite safe for you to leave your pup on the ground. Picking it up confirms its fear that other dogs are dangerous. This in turn may lead your dog to do the attacking when it is older, in the belief that it must get its bite in first.

Jumping up

Dogs that jump up can be discouraged by raising your knee so that they are pushed off balance as they do it. Always praise them once they have four feet on the ground again. Some adolescent dogs have the embarrassing habit of mounting people's arms or legs or even the furniture. This can be

Encourage your dog to be friendly

A raised knee will discourage jumping up

discouraged by pulling the animal off and slapping it across the flank. If you have taught your dog to lie flat on command, make it lie down until its excitement has subsided.

Leaving a dog

It should be possible to leave any dog without it making a noise. Here again it is much easier to start with a puppy. Shut it up in a room for a few minutes at a time daily, saying 'No' firmly through the door if it makes a fuss. As soon as it is quiet, even if only for a very short while, it should be let out and praised. If you are training a puppy in this way, do not go back into the room to correct it for making a noise, or it will begin to believe that it has only to bark for you to return. With an adult dog which has this bad habit, you will have to return to correct it.

Travelling and staying

Car journeys

Puppies should be introduced to car travel gradually by very short journeys at first. If, despite this introduction, the puppy is sick, make sure it is not fed immediately before a journey. Sometimes a drink of cold milk beforehand will help. If the dog is sick it should be offered glucose and water to help replace the fluid lost. You can buy proprietary travel sickness tablets, or a veterinary surgeon will prescribe medicine for a dog that suffers in this way. Finally, if you are uncertain whether your dog is going to be sick or not, a supply of plastic bags for the journey is a sensible precaution. If you time it properly, you can persuade your dog to be sick straight into the bag, thus preventing some messy clearing up.

Many dogs enjoy hanging out of car windows as they go along, but it is not really a kindness to allow them to do so because this habit can lead to eye trouble. If your dog has been taught to sit and stay, the training will prove very useful in a car, because the animal can easily be prevented from trampling over all the seats and the passengers.

Don't let your dog lean out of the car window

Make it wait for your command

Coming when called

A dog which comes when it is called under all circumstances
is a rarity. Even well-trained dogs are liable to feign deafness
when hunting something, or in the middle of an energetic
game. Puppies should be called to you frequently when they
are out, and praised and given a titbit. If you only call them
when you want to put them on the lead, they will eventually
connect coming with the end of freedom, and cease to obey.
Never call a dog to you when you want to correct it – always
go to the dog. Trying to grab a dog, or to catch it by running
after it, are both futile pursuits. In an emergency, if you call
the dog and then run away, it will often follow rather than
be left behind. If you have persevered in teaching your
dog to drop flat on command, a shouted 'Down' will sometimes succeed in stopping a dog in full flight that would
otherwise be deaf to the command to return.

Later training
Going to bed
It is very useful to have a dog that will go to its bed on command and stay there until told that it may leave. To teach this, as with any other command, you need perseverance and patience. Always use the same word for the same action, as inconsistency confuses the puppy. Repetition builds up the habit of obedience. Five minutes' practice twice a day is better than half-an-hour at one stretch. Put the dog in its bed, using the command 'Bed', and prevent it getting out until you tell it that it may. If you repeat this often enough, the dog will eventually obey on command alone.

Sitting and lying
The same process can be used to teach a dog to sit in one spot until released. While saying 'Sit', press the dog's haunches with one hand, and hold its head up with the other hand. Hold it in a sitting position until you release it with a word. Soon the dog will learn to sit on the command alone, and if

Many dogs enjoy performing simple tricks

you move away a step or two it can be prevented from following you by your voice alone. If it does move it must be put back in the same position, and the process repeated.

There are various methods of getting a dog to lie down, some of which are illustrated. It is, however, a knack more easily acquired with practice than explained on paper.

Learning tricks

Many dogs enjoy the attention they receive while performing tricks. A lot of these tricks are quite easy to teach, especially when you use food as an incentive. If you have taught your dog to sit, it is easy to embellish this by getting it to shake hands. Tell it to shake, and pick up its paw at the same time. Reward it with a titbit, and the idea will soon catch on. You can persuade it to offer each paw in turn. Begging is also taught from the sit position. Do not start this until the dog is at least six months old, because before this age the back muscles are not strong enough. Some dogs find it easier to learn to beg if they are sitting in a corner, so that the angle of the wall behind them helps them to balance.

A spaniel retrieving a pheasant

Fetching and carrying

Teaching a dog to fetch and carry objects can be easy or extremely difficult. Some dogs, in particular the retrieving breeds, take to fetching and carrying like ducks to water. Others cannot even be persuaded to take anything in their mouths, let alone to carry it any distance. If you have a dog that does not like carrying it is better to forget the idea and concentrate on things that it enjoys doing.

Training societies

If you are interested in having a well-trained dog, or have a problem animal, there are a large number of dog-training societies, with experienced trainers in charge. Here you will

A mongrel carrying a dumb-bell

see other dogs and can get advice. The address of your nearest society can be obtained from your kennel club.

Breeding
Looking after a bitch

A bitch will usually come into season first between the ages of six months and a year. During the period of being in season or 'on heat' she will be attractive to all male dogs, and will be ready and willing to mate. These periods last for approximately three weeks, and occur at six-monthly intervals throughout the bitch's life. The first signs are that the vulva (the external part of the genital orifice) begins to swell and exude a bloody discharge. In a short-coated breed this is immediately noticeable, but a careful watch needs to be kept with long-coated bitches because their long hair conceals it. From being hard and swollen, the vulva becomes softer and flaccid from about the ninth day onwards, and the discharge becomes colourless. At this stage the bitch will allow herself to be mated by any available dog. The discharge and the swelling both gradually disappear, until after three weeks things are back to normal.

If your dog is difficult, training classes can help

The need for vigilance

The care of a bitch in season requires constant vigilance. Even a normally obedient bitch may obey only her instincts at this time, and run off in search of a mate. Consequently, she should only be exercised on a lead and not left unsupervised, even in a supposedly dog-proof garden. Male dogs have a remarkable persistence and cunning, and mating has even been known to take place through a chain link fence.

Other dogs recognize a bitch in season by her smell. Masking the scent or deodorizing it helps to reduce unwanted attentions. You can obtain veterinary chlorophyll for this purpose, and strong-smelling liquids are also marketed. These can be sponged on the bitch's hindquarters, masking her attractive odour. The smell of the bitch, by the way, is unnoticeable to all but the keenest human noses. When exercising her, if possible carry her or take her a short distance by car at the start and finish. The break in scent will prevent dogs tracking her home.

Should accidental mating take place, a veterinary surgeon may be able to prevent an unwanted litter if the bitch is

Keep your bitch away from other dogs when she is in season.

taken to him straight away. It is also possible to have the bitch *spayed*, an operation that prevents reproduction altogether. Before considering this, however, remember that a spayed bitch cannot be exhibited under show rules. A veterinary surgeon will advise the best age for the operation.

The economics of breeding

It is not necessary for a bitch to have a litter for her health's sake, as is so often believed. Nor does a dog need to be mated for the same reason. If you do want your bitch to have a litter, you should consider the economics carefully. Mongrel puppies are valueless and are not economically worth producing. Even pedigree puppies can be remarkably difficult to sell at times. The amount an eight-week-old litter can eat is prodigious, and veterinary bills and stud fees all mean that the amateur is likely to get little profit.

A bitch should not be bred from during her first season, and should preferably be 18 months old or more. It is not wise to mate a maiden bitch over the age of five years.

Choosing a sire

If you have a pedigree bitch and wish her to have a litter, the choice of a champion sire will make the sale of the puppies much easier. Dog magazines carry advertisements of dogs at stud, and the breeder from whom you bought your puppy may be able to help with the choice of a sire. You pay a stud fee for the actual mating. Many stud dog owners will offer a free service at the bitch's next season should she prove not to be in whelp, but they are not obliged to. When your bitch comes into season, contact the owner of the stud dog of your choice, who will advise you as to the best day to bring her for mating. This is usually the tenth day from the beginning of her season.

Some technical terms

Although you may not be dealing with the mating of the two dogs yourself, it is as well to know the meaning of the terms used. The penis of the dog has a mass of vascular tissue at the base. When the penis is inserted into the vagina, the blood supply to this tissue is greatly increased, causing it to swell so much that it cannot slip out of the vulva. The locking together of the two animals like this is known as the *tie*. It can last anything from a few minutes to an hour. It is not, however, necessary for a tie to occur for the mating to be an effective one.

A simple, basic whelping box

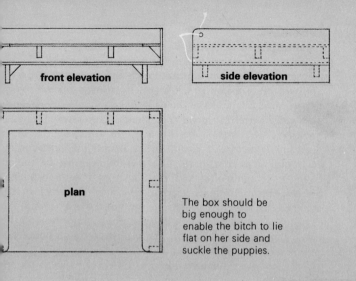

front elevation

side elevation

plan

The box should be big enough to enable the bitch to lie flat on her side and suckle the puppies.

The expectant mother

Even if your bitch has been mated, you should still take precautions to prevent any other dogs getting to her until her season is over. She should be treated quite normally for the first three weeks of her pregnancy. Thereafter, cod-liver oil and a mineral supplement should be added to her diet, which should be varied and plentiful. Gentle and varied exercise should be continued up to the day of whelping. With a small litter, it is often not possible to tell by the bitch's appearance whether she is in whelp or not. Often in the later weeks the nipples enlarge, and the movements of the puppies can be seen along the flanks of the bitch when she is lying on her side. A low-sided, roomy box makes the best whelping bed. If possible, a guard rail should be fitted inside the box, two inches up from the bottom and out from the side. Some inexperienced bitches are rather clumsy until they get used to motherhood, and a guard rail may save a puppy from getting squashed. The best bedding is probably newspaper. The box should be placed in a warm, secluded spot away from draughts and noise.

Whelping

From mating to whelping should take 63 days. The onset of whelping is indicated when the bitch becomes restless and refuses food. Her temperature drops, and the vulva enlarges. She will often make herself a bed by tearing up the newspaper. Most bitches have their litters easily, and interference does more harm than good. You should keep a watchful eye, however. Help should be given if, for instance, the bitch does not immediately clean off the membrane surrounding each puppy as it is born. The membrane must be pulled from the puppy's head to allow it to start breathing. Immediately after each puppy is born the afterbirth, which is still attached to the puppy by the umbilical cord, should be expelled. The bitch should clean the puppy, nip through the cord, and eat the afterbirth. She will then rough-house the puppy in a way that will both stimulate its breathing and its circulation. Some maiden bitches, however, appear so bewildered by the whole affair that they ignore newly-born *whelps* (puppies). Then the owners can step in to provide the necessary care that should have come naturally.

Newly-born puppies that appear to be dead should not be given up without endeavours to start their breathing

The whelp is born enclosed in a membrane with after-birth attached. The bitch should immediately remove the membrane to enable the whelp to breathe.

These should include rubbing with a warm, rough towel, and breathing gently into the puppy's mouth. Warmth is very necessary for youngsters at this stage, which is one of the reasons why it is difficult to persuade a bitch to leave her pups for even a few minutes in order to relieve herself. Some dog breeders use infra-red lamps to maintain the right temperature. The siting of such lamps needs care, and the manufacturer's instructions should be followed implicitly, as bad burns can result if the puppies came into contact with the lamp.

If you are worried by any phase of the whelping, contact your veterinary surgeon. He must be called if the litter is more than three days overdue; if excessive straining for more than two hours has not produced a puppy; or if the bitch appears in danger of exhaustion. Many veterinary surgeons like to see the bitch when whelping is complete, in order to give an injection which will ensure that all the afterbirth has been expelled. Some breeds are notoriously bad whelpers, in particular those with large heads and short muzzles. If you have a bitch of such a breed, you should consult a veterinary surgeon before the litter is due, and he can arrange to be on hand for the actual birth.

Warmth helps to revive new-born puppies

Examples of docked tails — Rottweiler and German Wire-haired Pointer

The litter

The nursing bitch should be fed lavishly and well. She may not want to eat for twenty-four hours or so after whelping, but you should offer her a drink of milk and glucose. Her diet, as well as being very nutritious, should also include some form of mineral supplement. Without such a safeguard, the bitch's supply of calcium may become so depleted as to cause fits, ending in coma and death.

The size of a litter depends very much on the breed, though generally the larger the dog the larger the litter. Eight puppies is the maximum a bitch should be expected to rear, and any above this number should be disposed of at birth.

Supplementary feeding is sometimes necessary, due to the failure of the bitch's milk or to the number of puppies. As a precaution, you should obtain a milk substitute and an eye-dropper before the litter is due. Hand-rearing orphan

Puppies can be hand-reared by using a medicine-dropper

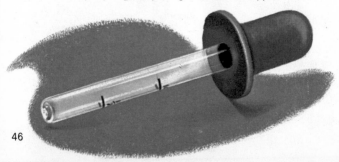

puppies is an arduous task. They need a temperature of between 85° and 90°F, and must be fed every two hours during their first week of life. After each feed, elimination must be encouraged by massaging the abdomen. It is natural for the bitch to eat the puppies' excreta in order to keep the nest clean. She may also regurgitate partially digested food for them when they are three weeks old or so and beginning to be weaned.

Claws and tails
Dew-claws should be cut off with sharp scissors when the puppies are two days old. Take the bitch away from the puppies first. Check first to see whether your particular

Kneading with their paws while suckling helps the milk flow

breed should have its dew-claws left on. In some breeds, such as Dachshunds, it is necessary for the front dew-claws to be left on. In others, such as Pyrenean Mountain Dogs, all the dew-claws are left.

If you have a breed which should have the tail docked, this should be done at the same time, but by a professional.

After the first week, you should check the puppies' claws. Cut off the sharp tips, because these can scratch and inflame the bitch's nipples. Between the ninth and the fourteenth days, the puppies' eyes open, and for a week or so after this they should be kept in dim light.

Weaning and worming

Weaning should be a gradual process. Start by offering the puppies warm milk when they are three weeks old. Add baby cereal, chopped, lightly boiled egg, cream cheese, and

(Red arrow) Mature worm lays eggs in the dog's intestines
(White arrow) Undeveloped egg is passed in its droppings
(Blue arrow) Egg develops further in the soil and may be ingested by another dog
(Blue arrow) The ingested egg now contains an embryo worm
(Blue arrow) The embryo worm hatches in the small intestines
(Yellow arrow) Now in the larval stage, the worm migrates through the liver, heart and lungs
(Yellow arrow) It is coughed up, swallowed, and reinfects the dog. When it reaches the intestine, it matures and starts laying eggs, which begins the whole cycle again.
The larvae can migrate through the blood system of a pregnant bitch to her developing puppies, and so the pups may be infected with roundworms at birth.

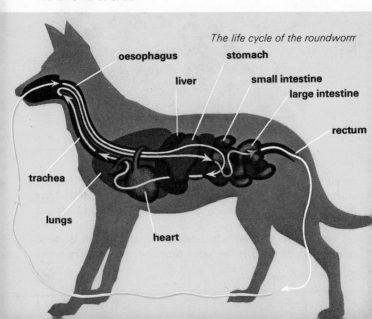

The life cycle of the roundworm

oesophagus
stomach
liver
small intestine
large intestine
rectum
trachea
lungs
heart

scraped raw meat to the diet as the bitch leaves the litter for longer and longer periods. At eight weeks the puppies are having five meals a day and are independent.

Worming should be done between the sixth and eighth weeks. Use proprietary worm pills for puppies, and follow the maker's instructions. As each puppy is dosed, put it in a separate place. It is surprisingly easy with a number of animals to forget which has had a pill and which has not.

Illness

The treatment of illness is the province of the veterinary surgeon, whose name, address, telephone number, and surgery hours should always be on hand. Any unusual behaviour may indicate trouble. Persistent scratching, general lethargy, persistent diarrhoea, continual shaking of the head or rubbing of the face on the ground, or an offensive smell are all symptoms that need investigation. A high temperature, bloody diarrhoea, an inability to pass urine, or fits (especially in nursing bitches) all need urgent treatment.

The first-aid cupboard for your dog

A first-aid cupboard should contain the following items:

Chlorophyll tablets for use with bitches in season, and for old dogs who by virtue of their age often smell strongly.

Worm pills for round worms. Other worms are best dealt with by a veterinary surgeon.

Golden eye ointment for the relief and treatment of minor eye infections.

Milk of magnesia for minor stomach upsets.

Clinical thermometer (blunt nosed) and some petroleum jelly to ease insertion.

It is essential to find the cause of persistent ear-scratching

A dog's temperature is taken in the rectum

Funnel and measuring glass.
Insect powder (make sure it is one for use on animals).
Disinfectant.

Taking temperatures

The temperature of a dog is taken in the rectum. It should normally be 101·5°. A temperature more than 1·5° above or below this needs professional investigation. To take the dog's temperature, first shake the thermometer down and smear petroleum jelly on the bulb. If possible, the dog should be held by an assistant so that it cannot sit down suddenly. Raise the tail of the dog and insert the thermometer into the rectum for about an inch for two minutes.

Giving medicine

It is easier to give liquid medicine from a small-necked bottle or through a funnel than from a spoon. Sit the dog in a corner, or stand behind it so that it cannot back away. Hold its mouth shut and its muzzle up. Pull out a corner of its lips so that a pouch is formed into which you can pour the liquid. As the liquid trickles to the back of the throat the dog will automatically swallow it.

To administer a pill, again get the dog sitting so that it cannot back away. Open its mouth and push the pill as far down its throat as you can. Close the dog's mouth and, holding its muzzle up, gently stroke its throat until swallowing occurs. Some wily dogs will hide a pill in their mouths, so watch carefully that your animal does not retreat to a corner as soon as it is freed and spit the medicine out. If it does, repeat the above procedure until you are certain the pill has been swallowed. Powders are easily given by sprinkling them on the back of the dog's tongue. It is also useful to remember that if you apply an ointment before the dog goes out for exercise, the excitement of the walk may very well encourage it to forget to lick the ointment off.

Stroking a dog's throat will encourage it to swallow a pill

Nursing and invalid diet

Keep a record for the vet of the dog's temperature, what it has eaten and drunk, and how often it has relieved itself. A puppy can often be persuaded to use newspaper when ill instead of having to be taken outside. If your dog refuses to relieve itself indoors, it must be well-wrapped up before being taken out. You should buy a ready-made dog coat, or make one yourself. The coat should protect the chest and abdomen as well as the back and flanks of the animal. The veterinary surgeon will probably advise about feeding the sick animal, whose appetite may well be non-existent. Milky drinks sweetened with honey and thickened with invalid food are nutritious and easily digestible. Chicken, rabbit meat, white fish, and lightly cooked eggs are all bland, nourishing foods.

Worms

Vermifuges are powerful drugs and should not be used unless there is actual evidence in the faeces. The only exception is that puppies should be treated for round worms at

A sick dog needs warmth and quiet

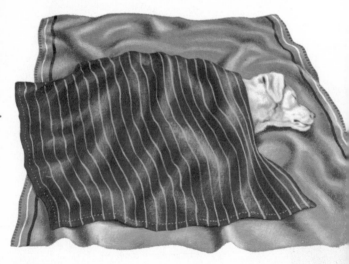

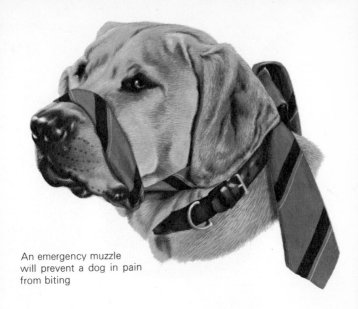

An emergency muzzle
will prevent a dog in pain
from biting

six to eight weeks, and again at four months. Round worms
are so called because they are round in section, about three
inches long, a dirty yellowish colour, and pointed at both
ends. In severe cases a dog will vomit worms as well as
passing them in the faeces. Heavy infestations of that nature
should be treated by a veterinary surgeon. Tapeworms are
more usually found in an adult dog than in a puppy, and are
best treated by a veterinary surgeon. The dog passes segments
of the worm, which look like pieces of greyish-white tape.

Injuries
It should be appreciated that a dog in pain or badly frightened
will snap at anyone within reach, even if it is someone it
knows well. Before attempting to help or move an injured
animal, tie its muzzle up to prevent anyone getting bitten. In
an emergency use a belt or necktie. If you suspect that the dog
has broken bones or internal injuries it should be slid on to
something rigid, such as a board, before being lifted. Even
using a coat held taut is better than picking the animal up in
your arms.

53

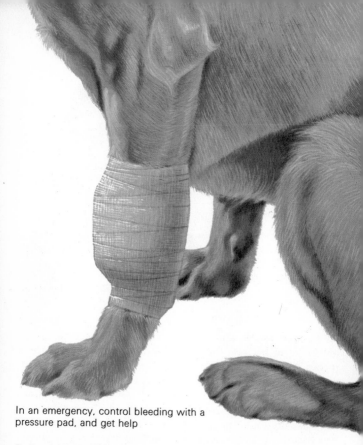

In an emergency, control bleeding with a
pressure pad, and get help

Pain and shock

For an animal in pain aspirin is a safe pain-killer. The dosage
is as follows: $\frac{1}{4}$ to $\frac{1}{2}$ tablet for toy dogs; $\frac{1}{2}$ to 1 tablet for
miniatures; 1 tablet for medium-sized dogs, such as spaniels;
2 tablets for dogs the size of Alsatians.

Shock can be caused by pain, fright or loss of blood. The
treatment is to keep the animal warm with blankets and
well-wrapped hot water bottles. The same treatment should
be followed in cases of collapse. Do not give liquids, as the
dog may choke. Burns and scalds should be covered. Apply
acriflavine ointment, give the dog an aspirin, and if severe,
treat for shock.

Fits, stings, bleeding and electric shock

Fits, hysteria, and convulsions are symptoms that need professional help. Keep the dog quiet in a darkened room, if possible sponging its neck and head with cool water, until the veterinary surgeon arrives. The same sponging treatment should be carried out for heat stroke.

Wasp stings occur quite frequently as dogs have a habit of snapping at these insects. Bathe the injury with a solution of bicarbonate of soda. If it is far back in the mouth, where swelling could interfere with breathing, get help.

Serious bleeding should be staunched by holding a pad firmly over the wound. As extensive loss of blood is serious, help should be obtained quickly.

Electric shock can occur if puppies chew wires. Sometimes the shock will cause the dog to pass a quantity of urine. Be careful not to step in this or touch the dog before disconnecting the current, as it can conduct electricity. Treat the dog for shock and burns if it is conscious. Artificial respiration can be tried if breathing has stopped. Squeeze the ribs firmly in time with your own breathing. You can try the 'kiss of life' method with small dogs.

Before applying artificial respiration, *remember to turn off the electric current*

Dog fights It is very difficult for one person to stop a dog fight without getting bitten. Dousing the animals with a bucket of cold water will sometimes shock dogs into letting go. If two people are present, grabbing the hind legs of the combatants and shaking them is often an effective deterrent

Length of life and inherited abnormalities

The length of life of a dog varies. Large dogs are often old by nine or ten, while a smaller breed may still be spry at twelve or older. Sooner or later, almost constant aches and pains and signs of senility make it kinder to ask the veterinary surgeon to ease your pet out of this life.

A number of inherited abnormalities have recently assumed alarming proportions in some breeds of dog. These include some forms of lameness and blindness. Unfortunately, these defects cannot usually be detected in young puppies and the exact way in which they are inherited is not always known. Veterinary surgeons and serious dog breeders are taking an increasing interest in the problems involved, with a view to eliminating the suspect strains.

DOGS AT WORK
Guards, trials and tests

Man has used dogs in innumerable ways for his pleasure and profit. A top-ranking show specimen can change hands for thousands of pounds or dollars. While show dogs are big business for some people, working and sporting dogs are still being used extensively in a variety of ways.

Police dogs

In Britain, the police use mainly Alsatians, with a few Labradors and Rottweilers. Roughly half the working strength consists of dogs given by the public. Handlers rear their own pups, and serious training starts at about nine months. As well as basic obedience, the dogs are taught tracking and man work. A police dog patrolling with its handler works a seven-hour day, and covers between 18 and 25 miles. The handlers are expected to try to vary the surface they patrol, as continual pavement pounding is bad for a dog's feet. Where this is not possible, police dogs tend to have a shorter working life than the average of six years. They are retired

The Alsatian, or German Shepherd Dog is the most popular for police work

gradually from active life and spend their old age as family dogs. Police in London trained Labradors to search for drugs. The dogs' sense of smell was so acute that they could detect heroin even in sealed containers.

In other countries, particularly Germany, the customs, railway police and border guards all use specially-trained dogs. As well as the breeds used in Britain, Airedales, Giant Schnauzers, and Dobermanns are on the payroll.

Working trials

In some countries, working trials to test dogs' working ability are held under the rules of the appropriate Kennel Club. These trials are a series of graded tests which include obedience work, agility tests, tracking and searching for concealed persons and hidden objects, food refusal and steadiness to gunshot. In Britain, dogs qualifying with high enough marks in the appropriate tests are entitled to the letters C.D. (Companion Dog), U.D. (Utility Dog), T.D. (Tracker Dog), or W.D. (Working Dog) after their names. A

Working trials in Britain require a scale jump

dog which wins two T.D. or W.D. Trials is entitled to the title of Working Trials Champion.

Obedience competitions

Obedience competitions are also held in many countries under the appropriate kennel club rules. The tests differ slightly from country to country but all the more advanced tests include heelwork, retrieving and scent discrimination. In Canada and the United States only purebred dogs are allowed to compete. Sufficiently high scores in three Novice, Open and Utility tests give the dog the right to the letters C.D., C.D.Ex, and U.D. respectively. Any dog having attained all these titles becomes an Obedience Trial Champion.

In Britain any dog is entitled to compete at Obedience Shows, whether it is pedigree or mongrel, provided it is listed on the obedience register at the Kennel Club. After the Novice class, Tests A, B, and C become progressively more difficult. Three outright wins of Test C at a Championship Show give the dog the title of Obedience Champion.

Tracking trials

Bloodhound breeders in Britain run their own tracking tests

Tracking tests are held for Bloodhounds

Dogs are trained to find people buried in snow

and tracking is included in the Working Trial's schedule. The American Kennel Club also runs its own Tracking Trials.

Rescue and research

The scenting powers of dogs have been used to rescue people lost or buried in snow. Just as a good sheepdog will indicate to the shepherd where sheep lie buried in drifts, so specially-trained Alsatians are used in the Alps to enable rescue teams to locate people trapped in avalanches. Mountain rescue teams in some countries, such as Britain, rely on a band of private owners with trained dogs, who are prepared to answer emergency calls. During World War I, Airedales and Collies were trained to find people injured in the bombing and guide rescuers to them. Ambulance dogs, which searched for the wounded were used by German and French armies.

The history of the use of dogs in war goes back to the pre-Christian era. In modern times, the Russians and the Germans have made the most use of trained dogs in the battlefield. The Russians have dropped dogs with their parachute battalions. Dogs have been trained successfully for mine detection. As well as guard and sentry duties, dogs have also been used as messengers, and have laid telephone cables across no-man's-land. More recently, the United States Army has been using dogs to assist patrols in jungle warfare, by detecting the presence of an enemy in thick cover and giving warning of ambush.

Dogs are being used in increasing numbers for medical research. The Russian physiologist Ivan Pavlov, in his classical investigations of conditioned reflexes, used dogs as the subject of his research. Dogs have also played an important part in the discovery of insulin. Investigation into the causes of rickets in Great Dane puppies led to the discovery of the factors which produce rickets in humans. Research on dogs led to the elimination of pellagra, a deficiency disease in humans. The Russian Sputnik dogs contributed to space research. The first of these was a Laika bitch fired in Sputnik II on 3 November, 1957. She perished in space after reaching an altitude of 1,050 miles. Two small Spitz-type dogs were launched into space in August, 1960. Their capsule circled the earth seventeen times and they were landed safely.

Russian dogs went into space

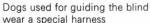
Dogs used for guiding the blind
wear a special harness

Guide dogs

The systematic and extensive training of guide dogs for the blind started in Germany in 1916. In Britain, the first guide dog training school opened in 1933.

Alsatians, Labrador Retrievers, Collies, and Boxers are all used as guide dogs, though Alsatians are in the great majority. A guide dog must not be aggressive, suspicious, or nervous, and must have initiative and a willingness to work. Only bitches are used, because they are generally temperamentally more suitable than males. Guide dogs are accepted between the ages of ten months and three years, and their training lasts four months. As well as simple obedience training, the bitch must learn to allow for the width and height of the person she is leading when going round obstacles. Traffic training consists of teaching the dog to understand that if a moving vehicle is within a certain area she must stop or deliberately disobey the command 'Forward', until the vehicle has either passed or is stationary. After the initial training period, the guide dog is introduced to her blind' owner, and the two spend a further four weeks at the centre, training together. The average working life of a guide dog is about eight years.

Circus dogs

Many dogs are natural showmen, and delight in the applause of an audience. Poodles are the breed most often used in acts, partly because of their intelligence, and partly because of their acrobatic abilities. It is very easy to teach a poodle to walk on its hind-legs, and poodles seem to regard being dressed up for their parts as a huge joke. A dog jumping through a hoop is shown on an Athenian jug of 500 BC. This may be the oldest dog trick in the world.

Circus dogs have universal appeal

Racing and coursing

Greyhound racing was first staged in Britain and the United States in the 1870s. Both ventures failed. Racing was revived in the United States in the early 1920s, with floodlit evening meetings. Its success there led to its revival in Britain in 1926. Big money gambled on the dogs attracted criminals, who tried to manipulate races to their own advantage. Their activities led to the formation of control bodies, and in all English-speaking countries these bodies operate on similar lines. In Britain, the National Greyhound Racing Club licenses tracks and officials, and registers all racing dogs. Each track has its own group of trainers. Owners who race their dogs on unlicensed tracks are warned off, and their animals are disqualified from racing. The National Coursing Club registers all greyhounds on a form that gives a very detailed description of colour and markings.

Graded races on licensed tracks are confined to dogs

kennelled and trained at the track where the race takes place. Open races can be entered by greyhounds trained at any licensed track, and those trained privately by licensed owners. The tendency in Britain is now for more long-distance races of 700, 900, and 1,140 yards, to replace the sprints of 400, 440, and 525 yards.

A racing greyhound may weigh up to 70 pounds. It can cover 440 yards in 22 seconds. Greyhounds start training at the age of 15 months. A healthy dog can be got running fit in six to eight weeks, and will lose four to six pounds in weight in the process. A good trainer treats each dog as an individual. But its life is short: a few find homes as pets when their careers are over, but most are destroyed.

In Britain alone, half a million pounds is gambled on greyhound racing every week. Top-class dogs can win thousands of pounds for their owners. Without a doubt greyhound racing is the biggest canine business in the world.

Racing Greyhounds wear a special muzzle

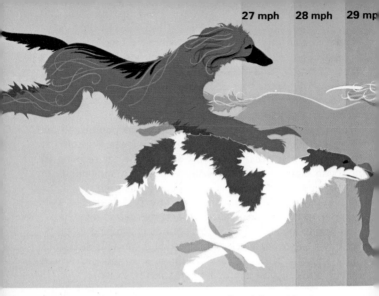

In order of speed the Greyhound comes first, followed by the Whippet, the Saluki, the Borzoi and the Afghan

The speeds of dogs
The speeds of running dogs are difficult to compare. One of the fastest times for the English Greyhound Derby course was clocked up by a dog called Pigalle Wonder at Wembley in 1958. Its speed was 37·76 m.p.h. A Saluki, however, is credited with achieving 43 m.p.h. Part of the difference must be accounted for by the fact that the Saluki was timed on a straight run, while the Greyhound was on an oval track. Salukis have been tried on greyhound tracks, but they refused to take an interest in the mechanical hare. As Salukis were bred for hunting gazelle, and gazelle can travel at well over 40 m.p.h., the Saluki's phenomenal speed may be true.

Greyhound coursing
The coursing of hares by Greyhounds takes place, in one form or another, in many countries. Owners of Borzois, Deerhounds, and Salukis also course their hounds. In Britain, Greyhound coursing is probably the oldest field sport. The rules were formalized in England by the then Duke of Norfolk

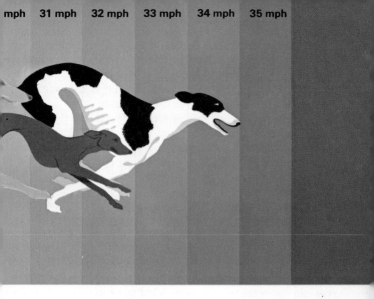

for Elizabeth I in the sixteenth century. Like Greyhound racing, coursing is controlled by a central authority in each country. In Britain, the contests are run on a knock-out basis. At a small meeting, the Greyhounds are walked up to within a certain distance of the hare. At a large meeting, beaters drive the hares towards the field where the Greyhounds are being held. The Greyhounds are drawn in pairs and the winner of each brace meets the winner of the next, until the last two dogs left meet in the final. Each brace of dogs is handed over to an official called a 'slipper' whose job it is to release the hounds simultaneously from a special leash called the 'slips' as soon as he meets a hare that will afford the dogs a good straight run. The hare has sixty to eighty yards start. A judge, riding horseback, decides the winner by reference to a code of points awarded for speed and turning ability. As Greyhounds hunt by sight, once the hare is out of sight the Greyhounds take no further interest in it. The dog that kills the hare is not necessarily the winner, and the majority of hares at a coursing meeting escape.

67

In 1836, an eight-dog contest was first run in Britain for a trophy called the Waterloo Cup. In 1857, this became a sixty-four dog contest. As such it has been competed for annually ever since. Similar contests, such as the Australian Waterloo Cup, are held in other countries.

Coursing also takes place in Eire, Portugal and the U.S.A., under their own authorities and rules. A modified form of coursing known as park coursing also takes place. This is held in an enclosed space from which the hare has no escape.

Whippet racing

Whippet racing, or *rag racing*, has recently been revived in Australia, Britain, and the United States. Rag racing got its name because the dogs were trained to race to an assistant, who stood shouting encouragement and waving a towel at the end of the track. Handicapping is now done on form, and the dog must start with all four feet on the ground. A Whippet can cover the two-hundred-yard track in twelve seconds.

The skill in Whippet racing lies in getting the dog to the peak of physical fitness at the right time.

Old-style Whippet racing died out after World War I, being superseded by the relatively cleaner sport of Greyhound racing. In the old-style races, Whippets were handicapped by weight. The races were started by the handlers launching their dogs up the track. The handlers could throw the dogs as much as five yards, so that they landed smoothly in their running stride. Deliberately starting a dog badly, or running an unfit dog so as to lengthen the odds at the animal's next race, were two of the dodges that got Whippet racing a very bad name.

Windhound racing takes place on the continent, principally in Holland, Germany and Belgium. This is strictly an amateur sport where owners race Whippets, Greyhounds, Salukis, Borzois and Afghan Hounds. These meetings are run by enthusiasts getting their enjoyment from entering their pet and show stock.

Coursing dates from the sixteenth century. The majority of hares escape and so scenes such as this are rare

The start of a hound trail in the North of England

Hound trails

Hound trails are becoming increasingly popular in many countries, particularly in northern England. Trail hounds were originally Foxhounds. Crossing them with Whippets and other breeds to give more speed without losing too much of the Foxhound's stamina, led to trail hounds being much lighter-boned, higher on the leg, and more racily built than a hunting hound is. In Britain, trail hounds are identified by ear tattoos. There is no handicapping, and the odds on the favourite winning are usually very short. Trail hounds are

privately owned and trained. The trail is laid by a man on foot, dragging a sack soaked in a mixture of kerosene (paraffin) and aniseed crystals. A puppy trail, for dogs born the previous year, covers five miles of steep fell country. The hounds must complete the course in fifteen to twenty-five minutes. If any hound takes less than fifteen minutes the trail is declared void, as the animal is assumed to have taken a short cut.

Adult dogs do a ten-mile trail in twenty-five to forty-five minutes. The trail is laid in a circle, so that the start and finish are almost at the same spot. As the trail layer comes walking back to the finish, the hounds are slipped to race past him on their way out. Finishing speed is all important, and as soon as the hounds come back in sight, their handlers start waving food and calling them home. Trail hounds may race twice a week during the season, so it is obvious that they are dogs with plenty of stamina as well as speed. This is also reflected in their relatively long racing life. Puppies start their training at six or seven months, and the animals may go on racing until six or seven years old. Though they are smooth-coated dogs, they are shaved before each racing season, and travel to each meeting rugged up like racehorses, in order not to catch cold before the start of the trail.

Hound trails also take place in the United States and other parts of the world

Carrying, herding, and retrieving

Dogs as transport

The use of dogs for haulage seems to have occurred only in Europe and lands in or near the Arctic Circle. In Britain the growth of traffic, the nuisance caused by the dogs' barking, and public sentiment against the use of draught dogs led to a law forbidding it in the mid-nineteenth century. Draught dogs are still used in decreasing numbers in some countries of continental Europe, and are usually adequately protected by law from exploitation.

Sledge dogs are still used quite extensively in the Arctic. There are three methods of harnessing them. A team of dogs can be harnessed in a line between two traces. There can be a single trace from the sledge, with pairs of dogs harnessed to it and a single lead dog out in front. In eastern Greenland, the dogs are fan-hitched, each animal being attached to the sledge by its own trace.

Sledge-dog racing is a popular sport in both Canada and Russia. Long-distance races over hundreds of miles test

A fan-hitched Husky team

strength and stamina. The record for the greatest load ever pulled by one Husky was set up by a dog named Charlie in Alaska in 1961. It shifted a sledge weighing 3,142 lb.

Shorter sledge-dog races are popular in Canada. Husky/ Alsatian or Husky/Collie crosses are used to give more speed. One of the most famous races is held in Quebec round a thirty-three mile course. Any number of dogs can be used in a team, but seven is the usual number, as more tend to slow the pace. The dogs haul a lightweight sledge weighing forty pounds, and the record for the course stands at one hour fifty minutes.

Truffle dogs

One of the more curious uses to which dogs have been put in Europe was hunting for truffles. The dogs were trained to sniff out the whereabouts of these edible underground fungi so that their owners could dig them out for sale. Truffle dogs were described as small, poodle-like animals, with white woolly coats. The breed is now extinct, and the dogs used in France and Italy are generally mongrel terriers.

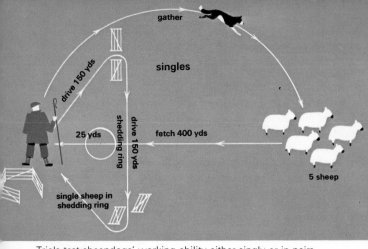

Trials test sheepdogs' working ability either singly or in pairs.

Sheepdog trials

Sheepdog trials are run in all parts of the world under the rules of the International Sheepdog Society. This was founded in Scotland in 1906. The home of the sheepdog trials was Wales, where they started in the early 1870s. The International Sheepdog Society did not become truly international until 1922, when an international championship competition was held with teams from England, Scotland, and Wales. The society was founded to improve the shepherd's dog, and establish a stud book recording sheepdogs' breeding. The trials consist of two tests, singles (for one dog) and doubles (for two dogs). Marks are awarded for a dog that works quietly, without fuss. A time limit is set, and any dog which bites a sheep is disqualified. The sheepdogs have to gather the sheep, fetch them to the shepherd, drive them between hurdles, separate out a marked animal from the rest, and finally pen the flock.

Field trials

Gundogs on the show bench are bred for their looks alone and are hardly ever used for their original work. In an effort to test the working abilities of gundogs, field trials were instituted. In America, these have become a highly popular competitive sport in their own right. Mainly trained by pro-

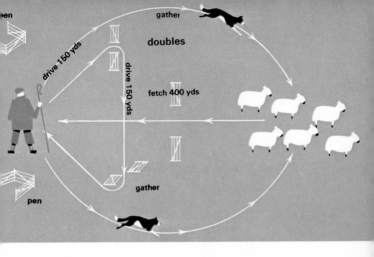

gather

doubles

drive 150 yds

drive 150 yds

fetch 400 yds

gather

pen

fessionals, some 60,000 dogs compete annually in the various trials. These are devised to test the various abilities of pointers and setters, spaniels, retrievers and the German pointing breeds. The judges mark the dogs for style, pace, nose and drive. A field trial dog is a specialist whose keenness demands a great deal of handling ability from his trainer. The successful field trial dog may not always be the best for an average shooting man. However, field trial dogs are much in demand for breeding, and their influence in this way is helping to raise the level of performance in ordinary working gundogs.

The well-trained gundog waits for the command to retrieve.

Foxhounds are followed on horseback

Hunting and fighting
Fox-hunting

Fox-hunting is a sport widespread throughout the English speaking world. It did not assume importance in Britain until the middle of the seventeenth century, when the disorders of the English Civil War broke up the deer parks and destroyed the big herds of deer. Before this, packs of hounds had hunted whatever came, including hares, wild boar, deer, foxes and wolves. Packs of hounds nowadays average between ten and twenty couples which may hunt up to three times a week in the winter hunting season. Good scenting powers and great stamina are essentials for a Foxhound, which may well cover more than twenty miles cross-country each hunting day.

Foxhunting takes place in Ireland and America, as well as Great Britain. American Foxhounds hunt the American red fox, a faster animal than the European fox. Packs of hounds are used all over the world for hunting various quarry. On the Continent hounds hunt foxes, hares, rabbits and deer. Jackals are hunted in South Africa and kangaroos are the quarry in Australia.

Beagles are followed on foot

Other hunting packs

Beagle packs are believed to be British in origin. They have been known in England since the time of Henry VII. They must hunt the hare painstakingly, and not so fast that they outrun the field, who follow on foot.

Harriers, as their name suggests, were also bred to hunt the hare. Smaller than Foxhounds, broader in the skull and coarser in the coat, Harriers are followed on horseback. Nowadays they often hunt foxes as well as hares. They are still hunted in Britain, Ireland, and America.

There are also some Basset Hound packs. Slower than Beagles, Basset Hounds also hunt the hare, and are followed on foot. These hounds are credited with the most beautiful of all hound music. Hunting Bassets are higher on the leg and less heavily boned than show specimens of the breed.

One pack of pure-bred Otterhounds exists in Scotland. These hounds have a wiry, water-repellent coat, and are noted for their perseverance, because water is not the best medium for following scent. Other Otterhound packs have a great deal of Foxhound blood in them. Otterhounds are more popular in America as show dogs.

Bets were laid on the number of rats killed in the shortest time

Stag-hunting

Stag-hunting was introduced into England by the Normans, but the true English Staghound no longer exists. Staghounds were the slowest and biggest of all hounds, being up to 30 inches at the shoulder. The last British pack, which hunted Exmoor, in south-western England, was sold to a German purchaser in 1825. Modern packs consist of large Foxhounds. Stag-hunting differed from every other sort of hunting in that the pack was divided into a small number of specialized hounds, known as *tufters*, and the main pack. Staghounds were taught to ignore all deer but the hunted quarry. The tufters separated the selected deer from the rest of the herd. When the stag had *gone away* (started running) the main pack was laid on. It is popular in many countries.

Dog-fighting

When bull-baiting was banned in Britain, dog-fighting became one of the more popular of brutal sports. The dogs used were the prototypes of the modern Staffordshire Bull Terrier. The fights took place in a dog pit about nine feet across, with a line marked across the centre. The first dog which failed to go across the line to tackle its opponent was the loser. Organized dog-fighting has been popular in many parts of the world, including America and the Far East. In Japan, fighting between crossbred Mastiffs was one of the recreations of the warrior caste.

Ratting and other activities

Another sport popular in the nineteenth century was to match two dogs in a pit to see which could kill a specified number of rats in the shortest time. A good dog – small terriers were used – would kill a hundred rats in less than ten minutes, and the record stands at five-and-a-half minutes.

From various descriptions that have come down to us it would appear that the dogs used to turn spits included short-legged terriers, bluish-grey dogs like the Cardiganshire Corgi, or bandy-legged animals with pendulous ears, like the Dachshund. Once the wheel was set in motion the dog could not rest.

The spit was turned by a dog running inside the wheel

The Boxer with natural ears as shown in Britain

DOGS ON SHOW
Kennel clubs

Nearly every country has its own ruling body in the pedigree dog world. Some countries have national bodies, such as the Kennel Club in Britain or the American Kennel Club. In other countries, such as Australia, each state has its own kennel club. Most European kennel clubs are affiliated to the Fédération Cynologique Internationale, and a number of other kennel clubs, such as those of Britain and India, are associated with it. The regulations of each vary in detail, but those of the British Kennel Club may be taken as typical.

In Britain, every dog has to be registered with the Kennel Club before it can be shown. Registration may be done by the breeder, or may be left for the subsequent owner of the dog to attend to. When a dog changes ownership, a transfer form must be sent to the Kennel Club for registration. In some countries, kennel clubs require very positive identifi-

The Boxer with cropped
ears as shown in America

cation of each dog. For example, in Canada a nose-print or an
ear tattoo is stipulated.

Every kennel club has its own list of breeds that it officially
recognizes. These lists differ, as a comparison between the
breed lists of the American and British Kennel Clubs shows.
For example, the King Charles Spaniel is known in the
United States, where it is called the English Toy Spaniel, but
the Cavalier is not recognized. The Americans divide Bull
Terriers into white and coloured varieties, but the Miniature
Bull Terrier, a British variety, is unknown. The British
Kennel Club recognizes several Tibetan breeds, but the
American Kennel Club only the Lhasa Apso and Shih Tzu.
The American list contains a number of working European
breeds unknown in Britain, which were taken back by
returning American Servicemen, or introduced by immigrants.

Show regulations

Kinds of shows

Dog shows are run under the rules of a country's kennel organization. In Britain, the largest shows are championship shows, of which Cruft's is the best-known example. These shows can be one-, two-, or three-day events. Challenge certificates are awarded to the best dog and bitch exhibited in each breed that is scheduled. An animal which gains three challenge certificates under three different judges at championship shows becomes a champion. The number of challenge certificates offered by the Kennel Club each year to each breed is proportional to the number of animals registered in that breed in the preceding years. The prize money offered at shows is not very great, but a good win can increase the value of a dog immensely. For this reason, the competition at championship shows is very keen.

Open shows are smaller in scope than championship shows, and are held more frequently. Championship shows

Pekinese are traditionally shown on a table in Britain

Exemption Shows in Britain have fun classes like this for the dog with the longest tail

and some open shows are *benched*. This means that wooden staging is erected, on which the dogs are displayed when they are not actually being judged.

Limited shows are those where the entry is restricted in some way, for instance to animals belonging to members of the society which is running the show. Sanction shows are the smallest kind. In such shows, young stock can be introduced to the show ring, and inexperienced owners can begin to learn the intricacies of presenting their particular breed.

Finally, there are exemption shows, which are usually charity events. By special permission from the Kennel Club the usual regulations are dispensed with, thus allowing novelty classes, such as the dog with the longest tail.

Entering for a show
In order to enter a show you must obtain a schedule from the show secretary. Read the small print carefully to find out for which classes your dog is eligible. The completed entry form and entry fees should reach the secretary before the closing date.

Various regulations

The system of showing varies from country to country. In the United States, for example, owing to the size of the country and the distance between shows, many more dogs are professionally handled. Brace and team classes are more popular than in Britain, and a dog becomes a champion on a points system. Shows over a certain size give a winning dog points towards its championship. Should the dog be a group winner, as well as 'best of breed', more points are awarded, while 'best in show' carries more points still. The exact number of points awarded varies with the breed entry. Fifteen points, awarded by three judges, give a dog its title.

New breeds and breed groups

The list of recognized breeds is continually growing, though the creation of new breeds is officially discouraged. In Britain, to be recognized by the Kennel Club a native breed must be proved to have been in existence for a hundred years or more. A foreign breed has to have credentials from the kennel club of its country of origin, or alternatively

Different breeds need different handling techniques

some documentary evidence of existence in its native land for a reasonable period. Each breed accepted like this is placed on the 'any other variety' register. If, over a three-year period, more than 150 dogs are registered, the Kennel Club transfers the breed to its officially recognized list and grants it challenge certificates. It follows that there are a number of breeds whose numbers do not warrant breed classes at championship shows, and which can only be shown in variety and rare breed classes.

In most countries, well over one hundred different breeds are recognized. For convenience of show administration the English Kennel Club has divided them into two groups – the sporting breeds, which are gundogs, hounds, and terriers; and the non-sporting breeds, which are utility, working and toy groups. In the descriptions of the. breeds that follow these groups have been adhered to. The heights given are the measurements of each dog from the ground to the withers (the ridge between the shoulder-bones). Heights and weights given are those for males, bitches being slightly smaller. The standards for some dogs specify height or weight only.

SPORTING BREEDS

The Gundog group

Gundogs were originally developed for finding or retrieving game. Now that the heyday of the gundog is over, some of the spaniel breeds are almost extinct.

Pointers

The function of a pointer in the field is to pick up the air scent of the quarry and freeze in position with its nose, body, and tail in a straight line pointing towards the bird. This characteristic is inborn in pointers and setters, but has to be brought out by specialized training.

The Pointer was probably originally developed in Spain, to find birds for falconry. When the breed was taken to England, it was given more speed. A Pointer needs a great deal of exercise, and is happiest when trained and working in the field. Its height is $24\frac{1}{2}$ in., and its weight is 50–55 lb.

The German Short-haired Pointer is not quite so racily built as the English Pointer, and has a coarser coat. The tail is docked to half-length. Its height is 25 in., and its weight is 55–70 lb.

The German Wire-haired Pointer is a versatile, rugged, and

Pointer

clever gundog, recognized in the United States but not in Britain. It is believed that it was evolved from the Pointer, the Foxhound and the Poodle. The wire coat is straight, harsh, up to two inches in length and is water-repellent. In the past fifty years it has risen to being the leading gundog in Germany, and is becoming increasingly popular for work in North America. Its height is 26 in.

The Wire-haired Pointing Griffon was introduced into the United States in 1900. It is a rare breed in Britain. The breed was created by a Dutch sportsman, Eduard Korthals, in the 1870s. As a result of Korthals' enthusiasm, the dog became quite well known, particularly in France. It is expected to find, point and retrieve game. The Wire-haired Pointing Griffon's coat is very distinctive, each individual hair of the top coat being harsh and stiff like thin wire. The dog is usually steel-grey in colour with brown patches. It has

German Short-haired Pointer

German Wire-haired Pointer

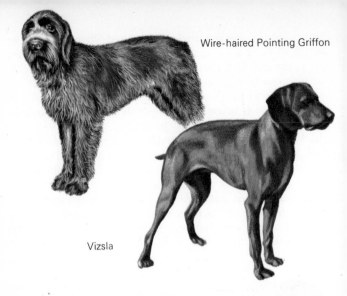

Wire-haired Pointing Griffon

Vizsla

something of a clownish streak in its character. Its height is
$23\frac{1}{2}$ in., and its weight is 56 lb.

The Hungarian Vizsla (pronounced 'veesh-la') is recognized
by the American Kennel Club, but is classified as a rare
breed in Britain. An all-purpose gundog, the Vizsla is
expected to find, point and retrieve game. Lightly-built yet
robust, it has a short coat, rusty-gold in colour. Its tail is
docked. Two world wars depleted the breed in Hungary,
but recently the Hungarian government has taken an interest
to ensure that only dogs of high standard are exported. The
dog's height is 24 in., and its weight is 70 lb.

Retrievers

The early nineteenth century saw the creation of several
breeds whose purpose was to locate shot game and fetch it
to hand. Before this time, retrieving had been one of the
things expected of pointers and setters. All the retrievers
inherit a good nose and a desire to fetch and carry.

The Curly-coated Retriever can be either liver or black.
There is a striking contrast between the smooth hair of the
forehead and muzzle, and the tight curls all over the rest of
the body. Its height is 22 in., and its weight is 70–80 lb.

The Flat-coated Retriever was pre-eminent during the early part of this century. Since then, for no very good reason, it has declined in numbers. This dog also can be black or liver. Its weight is 60–70 lb.

The Golden Retriever was created in the latter part of the nineteenth century and was mainly the product of Lord Tweedmouth's kennels. It is believed that Flat-coated Retrievers, a variety of spaniel now extinct, and the Irish Setter all helped to make the Golden Retriever. All shades of gold and cream are permissible, but not red. As it is a willing and intelligent dog of attractive appearance, it has maintained its popularity, despite a decline in the numbers used in the field. Its height is 24 in., and its weight is 65-70 lb.

The Labrador is the most widely-known and popular of the retrievers. Originally from Newfoundland, it is still used for field work, but has achieved new fame as a police dog and as a guide-dog for the blind. The Labrador's short, glossy coat is weather- and water-resisting, and can be

Curly-coated Retriever

Flat-coated Retriever

Golden Retriever

Labrador Retriever

Chesapeake Bay Retriever

black, yellow, or liver. Its height is 22 in., and its weight is
60–75 lb.

The Chesapeake Bay Retriever is an American breed unexcelled as a retriever for duck shooting. Its origins lie in
the story of two Newfoundland puppies which were rescued
from an English ship wrecked off the coast of Maryland in
1807. These puppies were later crossed with Otterhounds
and from their progeny eventually sprang the Chesapeake
Bay Retriever. Credited with fetching up to two hundred
ducks in a day from the rough, icy waters of Chesapeake
Bay, in eastern North America, this dog is tough both

mentally and physically. It is independent and stubborn in spirit, and rough going brings out the best in it. Its coat is short, thick, oily and wavy, and the colour varies from inconspicuous shades of dark brown to dead-grass. Its height is 26 in., and its weight is 75 lb.

Setters

The function of setters in the field is very similar to that of pointers. One of the breeds believed to have been used in the creation of all the setter family was the 'setting spaniel'. When it scented game, this spaniel crouched to the ground and crept up on the birds. Today, though their work with the gun has declined, setters continue to be popular because of their handsome appearance. They all need good exercise.

The English Setter combines great physical beauty and character with working ability. As a breed it owes much to Edward Laverack and Purcell Llewellin who improved its appearance and working ability in the nineteenth century. Its coat is slightly wavy, long and silky, with the legs well feathered. Colours are white with black, lemon or liver, or black, white and tan. Its height is 24–27 in., and its weight 56–66 lb.

English Setter

The Irish Setter is perhaps best known for its rich mahogany red colour. An hereditary disease of the eyes became very general in this breed in Britain during the 1940s, but concerted and courageous action by the breed club and the Kennel Club has almost completely stamped it out.

The Gordon Setter is the most powerful and the slowest of the three kinds of setters. Faithful and intelligent like the rest of the setters, the Gordon's loyalty makes it more of a one-man dog. Its colour is black and tan. Its height is 26 in., and its weight is 65 lb.

Spaniels

Spaniels did not really become distinct in type until this

Gordon Setter

century, although they are among the first dogs mentioned in English literature. Their function is to work through thick cover, flushing game for the guns.

The Clumber Spaniel was one of the first varieties of spaniel to be separately recognized, and takes its name from Clumber Park, in northern England, where it was developed. It is believed to get its low-slung appearance and reliable nose from an early infusion of Basset Hound blood. The Clumber's lack of speed is now a handicap when game is not so plentiful. Its height is 18 in., and its weight is 55–70 lb.

The Cocker Spaniel has achieved immense popularity as a pet. The reasons for the changes in fashion in dogs can only be guessed at, but the merry and willing character of the Cocker must have had a great deal to do with its rise in numbers. Originally bred to work fast through thick cover, the Cocker retains its desire to please. The great variety of colours in the breed must also account for part of its attraction. As well as the self colours – reds, blacks and goldens – parti-colours, tri-colours and roans are common. Its height is 15–17 in., and its weight is approximately 28 lb.

The American Water Spaniel and the Chesapeake Bay Retriever are the only two gundog breeds developed exclusively in the United States. Though the spaniel was recognized

Clumber Spaniel

English Cocker Spaniel

by the American Kennel Club only in 1940, it had been carefully bred as a working gundog for a long time. Its curly coat and compact build suggest Irish Water Spaniel and Curly-coated Retriever among its ancestors. It is a good water dog, excellent for flushing game and retrieving it. But its waterproof curls are a hindrance in some sorts of cover. Its height is 18 in., and its weight is 45 lb.

The Brittany Spaniel points its game instead of flushing it in the more orthodox spaniel style, and this, together with

Irish Water Spaniel

American Cocker Spaniel

its size, makes it more akin to a setter. Brittany Spaniels were first imported into the United States from France in 1931. Since then, the dog's hunting abilities have improved tremendously, and it is beginning to make its mark in field trials. The breed is not official in Britain. The dense, flat coat is orange and white or liver and white. Its height is $20\frac{1}{2}$ in., and its weight is 40 lb.

The American Cocker Spaniel differs in coat, size, and head qualities from the English Cocker. Exhibited in America since the 1880s, the divergence between the two types of Cocker Spaniel became so apparent that in 1936 the American

Kennel Club recognized the English Cocker as a separate variety. The American Cocker is divided by colour into three varieties – black; solid colour other than black (including black and tan); and parti-colour. The skull is more rounded than that of the English variety, and the coat is much more profuse. Its height is 15½ in., and its weight is 28 lb.

The Field Spaniel is a British-developed spaniel whose origin is closely linked with that of the Cocker Spaniel. It has gradually evolved through several crosses – probably Basset Hounds – to a longer-bodied, heavy and low-to-ground dog. Since the last century Field Spaniel backs have

Field Spaniel

been shortened and a little weight taken off, until the breed now almost resembles a stoutly-built Cocker Spaniel. It is not a widely favoured breed among shooting-men, although, being larger than the Cocker, yet more active than the Clumber, it is surprising that it has not been more popular. Today, it is little seen either in the field or on the show bench. Its colours can be black, the most usual, black and tan, liver, liver and tan and liver roan, though all colours are permitted. Its coat is flat, close-fitting and silky. Its height is 16–18 in., and its weight is 35–50 lb.

The Irish Water Spaniel, like the Wolfhound, is one of the oldest of breeds. It was probably taken to Ireland from the East through Spain more than 2,000 years ago. There is no other breed like it in its distinctive appearance and enjoyment of water work. Never a numerous breed, even in its own country, the breed has steadily progressed by sheer hard work on land and water. With the Chesapeake Bay Retriever, the Irish Water Spaniel is the most popular duck-dog in the lowland States of America. It is reputed to have an independent and humorous nature, but its oily coat has probably prevented it from becoming more popular as a pet. Its colour is rich, dark liver and its coat consists of dense, tight and crisp ringlets all over the body except the face, fronts of legs and tail. Its height is 21–23 in. and its weight is 50–65 lb.

The English Springer Spaniel is considered one of the ideal breeds for a rough-shooting man who requires a reliable all-round worker. Being an active, keen dog, larger than the Cocker, the English Springer will retrieve all kinds of fur and feather, as well as flushing game from the thickest cover. Animals of this breed have many successes in field trials to their credit. In the Middle Ages and Elizabethan times, spaniels were used to locate game and flush the birds for

English Springer Spaniel

Welsh Springer Spaniel

Sussex Spaniel

Weimaraner

falcons to catch. From this comes the name 'springer'. Another type of Spaniel was taught to crouch when scenting game and remain quietly while it was netted. These dogs, which were called 'crouchers', are believed to have been used in the creation of the modern setter. The English Springer is usually liver and white. Its height is 20 in., and its weight is 40–50 lb.

The Welsh Springer Spaniel is slightly smaller than its English relative, and not so well-known outside its native Wales. Its red and white colouring and its smaller ears also distinguish it from the English Springer, whose working ability it shares. Its weight is 35–45 lb.

The Sussex Spaniel was purposely bred low-to-ground in order that it might push its way under the bramble thickets of its native English county. Slow and conscientious as it is, it is out of favour with shooting men owing to its habit of giving tongue when working through cover. The colour should be a rich, golden liver. Its height is 16 in., and its weight is about 45 lb.

The Weimaraner (pronounced 'vi-mar-aner') is a breed

created in Germany in the early nineteenth century as a hunting dog capable of dealing with such quarry as wolves, deer and wild cat. One of the old French hounds gave it its distinctive coat colour, and Bloodhound crosses gave it its nose. The Weimaraner was taken from Germany to the United States in 1929, but did not become known in Britain until the 1950s. Great attention has always been paid to the breed's working ability and temperament. Its amber eyes and mouse to silver-grey colour give it a remarkably distinctive appearance. Its height is 22–25 in., and its weight 45–65 lb.

Hounds

The hound group of dogs is really made up of two different types of animal, the scent hounds and the sight hounds. The scent hounds are generally long-eared, with domed skulls and heavily-boned muscular legs. The sight hounds are built for speed and agility. They are long and lean from muzzle to tail, and have tucked-up bellies and deep chests. Though generalizations are misleading, hounds are more independent and wilful than the affectionate, biddable gundogs.

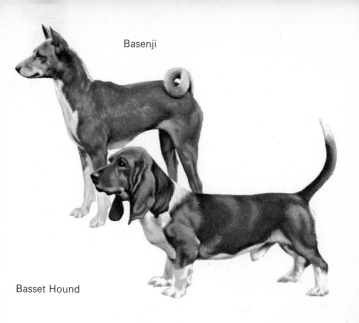

Basenji

Basset Hound

The Afghan Hound can claim one of the longest recorded histories of any breed, being first mentioned in ancient Egypt in the period 3000 BC. How the dogs got from there to Afghanistan we do not know, but the breed became established in Britain after World War I, when it was taken back by returning British Army officers. Used for coursing game in mountainous country, the Afghan is believed to be the fastest hurdler of all the hounds. Legend has it that Afghans were the dogs that Noah took into the Ark. The dog's height is 27–29 in., and its weight is about 64 lb.

The Basenji is a native of central Africa. It comes from the Congo, but relatives of similar general appearance are widely spread throughout the length of the Nile. They were known in ancient Egypt, and were used then for their hunting ability, as they are in Africa today. Although the Basenji's appearance is so different from that of other hounds, it too possesses a wonderful nose. Possibly the breed's most famous characteristic is its inability to bark. However, it is very far from silent, as it produces a wide variety of yowls and chortles. The wrinkled forehead, the tightly-curled tail, and the running gait are typical. The colour should be bright red and white, or black and tan and white. Its height is 17 in., and its weight is 25 lb.

The Basset Hound is becoming very popular as a show dog and a pet. It was first imported from France to Britain in 1866. Although low to the ground, it is a heavily built dog. It has a mind of its own and requires plenty of exercise. The wrinkled head, resembling that of the Bloodhound, and the long velvety ears are very attractive. Its height is 14 in.

The Beagle is another hound breed now becoming very popular as a pet. It was for a number of years the most popular breed in the United States, and the smaller American type of dog is now preferred in Britain. The Beagle may very well be the oldest British breed. It has certainly been hunting in Britain as far back as there are records. The handy size, smooth coat, and gay appearance of the Beagle must all contribute to its present popularity. Its height is 13–15 in.

The Bloodhound is another breed which has been known for centuries. Its remarkable scenting powers have been used to advantage in the creation of many other breeds. It is too big for urban living, and has a quite unwarranted

Bloodhound

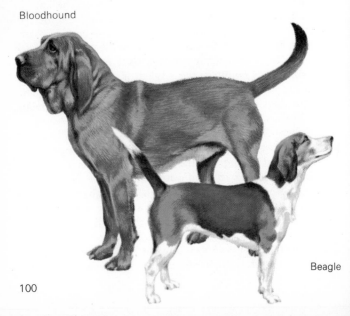

Beagle

Black and Tan Coonhound

Borzoi

reputation for ferocity. In actual fact, that heavily wrinkled brow that appears so careworn hides a retiring and gentle dog. Its height is about 26 in., and its weight is 80–90 lb.

The Borzoi, or Russian Wolfhound, is one of a group of coursing hounds, which include the Deerhound and the Saluki, all bred for speed. The breed's early history is of a dog kept solely by the Russian aristocracy and used by them for coursing wolves. The hounds were held in pairs at strategic points round a thicket known to contain a wolf. When the quarry was flushed, the nearest brace of hounds was slipped to bring the animal down. The Russian Revolution of 1917 brought an end to the large aristocratic kennels, but by then the breed was becoming established in Britain and the United States. The long silky coat can be any colour, and the height should be at least 29 in.

The Black and Tan Coonhound is a peculiarly American

Smooth-haired Dachshund   Long-haired Dachshund

breed. Produced from a cross between the American Foxhound and the Bloodhound, the Coonhound is a slow worker
with a fine nose, and is specially trained to track and drive
raccoons and opossums up trees. The colour must be black
with bright tan markings. Its height is 27 in.

The Dachshund exists in six varieties. The breed is a very
old German one, and was originally bred to hunt the badger,
the word *Dachshund* being German for *badger dog*. Bred low
to go to ground, the Dachshund was required to bay the
badger, indicating by much barking where the badger was
holed up so that it could be dug out by the hunters. The
German Dachshund Club still runs trials to test its gameness
and willingness to go to ground. Active and independent in
character, Dachshunds first became favourites in Britain
when Queen Victoria had one as a pet.

Wire-haired Dachshund

Miniature Smooth-haired Dachshund

THE SMOOTH-HAIRED DACHSHUND has always been the most popular. The coat should be short, dense, and smooth, and can be any colour except white. Reds and black and tans are common, with chocolates and dapples being more unusual. The body should be as long and low as possible and the weight should not exceed 25 lb.

THE LONG-HAIRED DACHSHUND is believed by some people to be the oldest of the varieties in its native country. Similar in shape and size to the standard smooth, its coat should be soft and long, slightly wavy and shining.

THE WIRE-HAIRED DACHSHUND was produced in Germany in the eighteenth century. Its short, thick, wiry coat, with its bushy eyebrows and beard, distinguish it from the other varieties. In Britain it has never quite attained the popularity of the other two.

Three miniature varieties are now becoming even more numerous than the Standards. These are Dachshunds under 11 lb. in weight, but having the same coat textures as the three standard types.

The Scottish Deerhound is one of the oldest breeds in the British Isles. It was developed to course deer in the Highlands of Scotland and nearly became extinct after the introduction of the quick-firing rifle, and after the dispersal of the Highland chiefs following the defeat of Prince Charles Edward Stuart at Culloden in 1746. Enthusiasts restored the hound, and the artist Landseer and the novelist Sir Walter Scott did much to popularize it. Although the deerhound's great size means that only a minority can afford to keep it, the nobility of the breed is such that its numbers remain fairly constant. A thick, close-lying, harsh somewhat ragged coat is required, with a moustache of silky hair. Its height should be not less than 30 in., and its weight 80–105 lb.

The Norwegian Elkhound, a member of the Spitz group, is a modern example of a type of dog that has been in existence in northern Europe since 4000 BC. It is mentioned in the old Norse sagas, and its remains have been found buried with the Vikings and their weapons. It has always been used as a hunting dog in Scandinavia, at first for hunting bear, and,

Scottish Deerhound

Norwegian Elkhound

Finnish Spitz

when these became scarce, for hunting elk. Either the hounds are let loose to track the elk and bring it to bay or, more usually, they are leashed and lead the hunter to his quarry. It was introduced into Britain in the 1870s, but did not gain popularity until later. The Elkhound's popularity as a pet is due to the fact that it is both versatile and adaptable. It is a compact dog, with a thick, hard, weather-resisting grey coat. Its body is short and strong, with a tightly curled tail. Its height is 20 in.

The Finnish Spitz is another member of the northern group of Spitz breeds and has been bred in Finland and Lapland for centuries. It has the typical sharp-pointed muzzle, erect ears, and short back, and has a bushy tail curled over the hindquarters. Used by the Finns as a bird dog, it is still used as a gundog in its native land. Its reddish brown coat increases its likeness to a fox. It is not recognized in the United States. Its height is 16–19 in.

The English Foxhound is a beautiful example of an animal whose appearance has been moulded through the centuries by careful breeding for pace, nose, and stamina. Hardly ever kept as companions, Foxhounds are very rarely seen at dog shows. The English hunting hounds have their own hound shows. The coat is generally white, black, and tan, or lemon and white. The dog's height is approximately 23 in., and its weight is 70 lb.

The American Foxhound is much more diverse in type than the English Foxhound, as it is used for a number of different purposes other than the pursuit of foxes followed by horsemen. There are drag hounds, corresponding to the British fell hounds, competitive field trail hounds – which need speed and a rather jealous nature – and also a slow type of hound with a good voice, used by those interested in hunting the fox with a gun. The English variety was first taken to America in about 1650 and from this and later importations

English Foxhound

American Foxhound

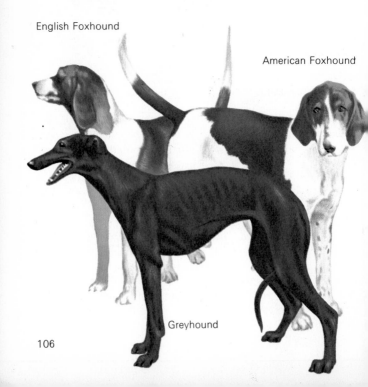

Greyhound

Harrier

Ibizan Hound

the various strains of American Foxhound were developed. Its height is 22–25 in.

The Greyhound is in a minority as an exhibition dog, because far more Greyhounds are kept for racing and coursing than are kept for show. The show dog is not quite so fast as the track sprinter, chiefly because its hind angulation differs from that of the racing dog. Its height is 27 in., and its weight is 50–55 lb.

The Harrier is smaller and slower than the Foxhound. The pure-bred Harrier is rare in Britain but not in the U.S.A., where it is used for drag hunting. Its height is 18–19 in.

The Ibizan Hound is a Spanish breed from the Balearic Islands, where it has been kept remarkably pure. It is very similar to the dogs shown in the mural paintings of ancient Egypt. A fairly large, powerfully built type of greyhound, the Ibizan has erect, mobile, bat ears. The preferred colour is red. This hound has an excellent nose, and the Spaniards use it either singly or in a pack for hunting rabbits or hares. Its height is 26 in. and its weight is 50 lb. Rare in Britain it is unknown in the U.S.A.

Irish Wolfhound

Otterhound

Whippet

The Irish Wolfhound is another of the ancient and majestic sight hounds. Early Irish literature contains many references to the breed but with the extinction of the Irish elk and the Irish wolf, the numbers of Wolfhounds declined. There is a certain similarity to the Deerhound, but the Irish dog is bigger, heavier, and more powerful. Like most very large breeds, the Irish Wolfhound is a quiet and dignified animal and a loyal companion to those who can afford to keep it. Its coat is rough and hard; its head long with powerful jaws. It has small ears, a racy body and a long tail. Its height should be at least 32 in., and its weight is 120 lb.

The Otterhound is the product of the Southern Hound, Bloodhound, Griffon Vendéen and the Welsh Hound. It is not common either in Britain or the United States. There are few pure-bred hounds in England, and only one pure-bred pack in Scotland. In the United States, the Otterhound is used for general sport. It should have a harsh, crisp, oily top coat, with a woolly undercoat to resist the wet. Its height is 24 in., and its weight is 65 lb.

The Rhodesian Ridgeback was evolved by South African Boer farmers to guard their farms against intruders, hunt practically any quarry, and withstand the sudden and great

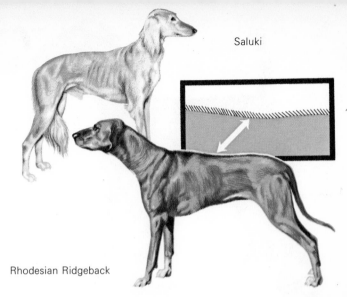

Saluki

Rhodesian Ridgeback

changes of temperature of the veld. Later it was imported into Rhodesia, where it was used to bring lions to bay, thus earning the nickname of 'lion dog'. Its most distinctive feature is the ridge of hair growing along the spine contrary to the direction of the rest of the coat, which is short and dense, sleek and glossy. It is fearless and intelligent. The colour is light to red wheaten. Its height is 27 in., and its weight is 85 lb.

The Saluki is a variety of Eastern Greyhound, pure-bred by the Arabs for many generations. The Saluki has been used for centuries from Persia to the Sahara for coursing gazelle and smaller game. It was introduced into Britain in the last century. The soft, silky coat adds a final touch of elegance to a dog built for speed and running over rough country. Its height is 23–28 in.

The Whippet is known as 'the working man's greyhound' in Britain. It is still extensively raced. As a companion, it is affectionate and intelligent, with a fine, short, close coat that needs little attention. Resembling a typical Greyhound in miniature, the Whippet can be any colour or mixture of colours. Its coat is fine, short and close. Its height is $18\frac{1}{2}$ in. and its weight is 21 lb.

109

Airedale Terrier

Terriers

The Terriers as a whole are a group of dogs distinguished by their gameness of temperament. Alert, hardy and energetic, as their name (from the Latin *terra* meaning earth) suggests they were first developed to follow their quarry, whether fox or badger, underground. They were later used for killing any vermin. It is only in the past hundred years or so that pure breeds have been recognized and established. Before that, local types were produced, because a dog admired for its working ability would sire many puppies in its own neighbourhood. This is why the names of many terrier breeds are those of places. Ideal dogs for those who admire spirit, some can become too noisy or too aggressive unless firmly checked when young. Hunt terriers, small enough to be carried on horseback and game enough to bolt a fox for the hounds, have given rise to a number of recognized breeds such as Border and Sealyham Terriers. Small, short-legged, white terriers with a pied patch on the head are sometimes offered for sale as Jack Russell Terriers. The name arose because an Exmoor cleric of that name bred a distinctive wire-haired terrier to run with his hounds at the beginning of the nineteenth century. None of his strain survived. The name lingers on to describe small, game mongrel terriers.

The Airedale is the largest of the terriers, and therefore known as the 'king of terriers'. It takes its name from the valley of the Aire in Yorkshire and is less excitable than most terriers. It has been used for big game hunting, police work and as a war dog, but is nowadays chiefly valued as a companion and guard. Its hard, wiry coat should be black or dark grizzle and tan, and the tail is docked. Its height is 24 in., and its weight is 48 lb.

The Australian Terrier is one of the very few terrier breeds not developed in Britain. It is descended from the Yorkshire, Norwich, Cairn and other British terriers. It was manufactured in Australia in the 1880s, and for a long time the breed remained very diverse in type. One of the smallest of the working terriers, it should be bold and cheerful. The dog has a soft top-knot of hair, but the rest of the coat should be straight, harsh and about two inches long. The colour should be either blue and tan or sandy-red. Its coat is straight and hard, its ears pricked or dropped forward and its tail is docked short. The dog's height is 10 in., and its weight is 10–11 lb.

Australian Terrier

The Bedlington Terrier is one of the oldest terrier breeds to be clearly defined, having certainly been in existence since the early 1800s. It developed in Northumberland and is akin to other terriers of the Border Counties such as the Dandie Dinmont. Unlike any other terrier in appearance, the Bedlington shares the terrier reputation for gameness. Unfortunately, the dog's shape, and the soft linty coat which gave it the appearance of a lamb, meant the animal often became a pampered pet, and some of the original fire has been lost. Blue is the colour most often seen, though liver, and either colour with tan, are also permissible. Its low set ears have a fringe at the tip. Its height is 15–16 in., and its weight is 18–23 lb.

The Border Terrier was unknown outside the Border districts of England and Scotland until granted breed status by the English Kennel Club in 1920 and by the American Kennel Club in 1932. But it was in existence by the end of the seventeenth century. It has to be large enough to follow a horse, and small and courageous enough to bolt a fox from

Bedlington Terrier

Border Terrier

Bull Terrier

its earth. One of these dogs, despite being badly mauled, is reported to have killed a badger single-handed, which is no mean feat for a dog of any size. It is a sensible, unexaggerated shape, and needs neither trimming nor docking. Its colour should be red, wheaten, grizzle and tan, or blue and tan. Its coat is harsh, weather-proof and with a good, thick undercoat. Its height is about 12 in., and its weight is 13–15½ lb.

The Bull Terrier. An extract from the British Bull Terrier Club's standard states that 'the Bull Terrier is the gladiator of the canine race . . . full of fire, of sweet disposition, amenable to discipline'. The breed as we know it today was created in the 1850s. An all-white dog was bred from the Bulldog and from terrier crossbreds used for dog-fighting and ratting. There are neither height nor weight limitations, but a dog with maximum substance for its size is required. Its colour can be pure white, white with markings on the head, or 'coloured', i.e. brindle or black to predominate. Its coat is short and smooth. Miniature Bull Terriers are recognized in Britain as a separate variety, being under 14 in. in height and 20 lb. in weight.

Cairn Terrier

The Cairn Terrier is another of the small working terriers that are too sporting and game in character ever to enjoy being lap-dogs. They come from Skye and the Western Isles of Scotland, where their job was to bolt foxes, martens and wildcats. The head of a Cairn should be broader than that of the other small terrier breeds, and a dark mask is desirable. Its coat should be profuse and harsh with a close, furry under-coat, and can be any shade except white. Its tail is quite short and carried gaily. The dog's height is 10 in., and its weight is 14 lb.

The Dandie Dinmont Terrier is a dog handy in size and big in character that deserves to be better known. Named after a character who owned a pack of these sporting terriers in Sir Walter Scott's novel *Guy Mannering*, it is another

Dandie Dinmont Terrier

Smooth-haired Fox Terrier

Wire-haired Fox Terrier

tough, vermin-killing terrier from the Border country of Scotland. Its domed head should be covered with soft, silky, light hair, while the rest of the coat is crisp to feel, rather than hard and wiry. Its body is long, low and muscular and its colour should be either pepper, dark bluish-black to silvery-grey, or mustard, reddish-brown to pale fawn. Its height is 8–11 in., and its weight is 18 lb.

Smooth- and Wire-haired Fox Terriers, though recognized and shown as two varieties, may be considered together, as in conformation they should be identical. Still at times used for fox bolting, they should be small enough to enter a fox-earth or drain yet large enough to run with hounds. Always popular, the Fox Terrier is predominantly white in colour with black or tan markings. Gay and lively, it can be rather noisy unless checked. The wire coat should be dense and crinkly like coconut matting, and needs expert trimming to maintain its texture and show off the dog's appearance. The 'hound-marked' dog is much admired, and its tail is docked. The Fox Terrier's height is $15\frac{1}{2}$ in., and its weight is 16–18 lb.

The **Irish Terrier** is a fighting breed which inspires intense loyalty among its devotees. They were originally used for sporting purposes and were frequently matched against each other in fights. The breed was first exhibited in 1870 and from then on became increasingly popular in England and the U.S.A. Known as 'the red devil', it is a taller, racier terrier than the Fox Terrier, with whole coloured, wiry coats of any shade of red. Though a hard-bitten and sporting character, it is very sweet tempered and loyal to the human race. Its general appearance is lithe, wiry and very powerful. Its height is 18 in., and its weight is 25–27 lb.

The **Kerry Blue Terrier** is the largest of the Irish terriers, and has the fiery temperament of the Irish Terrier. Distinct as a breed in Co. Kerry, Ireland, in the nineteenth century (probably being descended from the Gadhar, an extinct type used by the ancient Irish for sheep-herding) the Kerry Blue

Lakeland Terrier

Kerry Blue Terrier

Irish Terrier

first appeared in England in the 1920s. It is an all-round working terrier, having been used in its time for everything from sheep-herding to killing vermin. The coat should be profuse, soft and wavy with an abundant forelock. In puppies it is almost black, sometimes with tan points, but this changes to the blue of the adult coat. Its head is long and lean with a flat skull, strong jaw and foreface. Its body is strong, muscular and well-proportioned. The dog's height is 18 in., and its weight is 33–37 lb.

The Lakeland Terrier, as its name suggests, is another breed whose origins were with the packs of Foxhounds and Otterhounds in Cumberland and Northumberland, in northern England. Bred first of all for gameness, the Lakeland started to appear at shows after World War I, and achieved championship status in Britain in 1931. It has a smart, workmanlike appearance which has made it popular as a companion. Its harsh, weather-resisting coat is most often black or blue-and-tan, or red grizzle. Its head is well balanced with a flat skull, powerful jaws and broad but not overlong muzzle. Its tail is docked. Its height is $14\frac{1}{2}$ in., and its weight is 17 lb.

Manchester Terrier

Norfolk Terrier

The Manchester Terrier had its heyday at the end of the nineteenth century. Originally descended from black-and-tan ratting terriers, the Manchester was probably crossed with a whippet to give refinement. The Kennel Club's ban on ear cropping caused a severe drop in the Manchester's numbers in Britain, as many of the older fanciers would not tolerate the small drop ears that are now part of the standard. In the United States the breed is still usually shown cropped. Its smooth, lustrous coat is jet-black, with rich mahogany tan markings, and is close, smooth, short, glossy and of firm texture. Its tail is not docked. Its height is 16 in., and its weight is about 16 lb.

Norwich and Norfolk Terriers are described together here, as the only difference between them is in ear carriage. They are all known as Norwich Terriers in U.S.A., but in 1964 the British Kennel Club gave permission for the two varieties to divide, the drop-eared dogs being known as Norfolk Terriers and those with erect ears as Norwich Terriers. They are descended from some small Irish Terriers used in Norfolk for fox and badger working, probably crossed with other British hunting terriers and bred to size. They are independent, sporting and stockily-built dogs, with short legs, a wire coat, and the true terrier personality. The dog's height is about 11 in., and its weight is 12 lb.

The Scottish Terrier. The popularity of the black Scottish Terrier is such that few of the general public realize that both brindle and wheaten are also permitted colours. It is an ancient breed used centuries ago for sporting purposes. The Scottish Terrier is one of the most widely kept of the terrier breeds, its sturdy loyalty and gameness making it many friends. It is one of a group of working terriers from north of the England-Scotland Border, including the Skye, Cairn, Dandie Dinmont, and West Highland White, whose origins are very much mixed. The modern Scottie needs a good deal of trimming and the exaggerated body shape is beginning to lead to whelping difficulties. Its coat is wiry, of medium length. Its head is fairly long with ears small and erect. Its back is short, its tail thick at the base, tapering and gay. Its height is 10 in., and its weight 22 lb.

Norwich Terrier

Scottish Terrier

The Sealyham Terrier was named after 'Sealyham', the country estate in southern Wales where, in the 1850s, its owner, Captain John Edwardes, created a short-legged, rough-haired terrier capable of facing any kind of vermin. He tested the courage of his dogs on polecats, and any who hesitated to go into the kill he destroyed. Since reaching the show ring in about 1910, the Sealyham Terrier has become much more standardized in type and much lower to the ground. It is tremendously popular in the U.S.A. Its wiry coat is white with markings permitted only on the head. Its height is 12 in., and its weight is 20 lb.

The Skye Terrier is an old breed, descriptions of it date back to the sixteenth century. For over 30 years Queen Victoria maintained a keen interest in it and through this helped make it popular. Its long coat has always attracted attention, and is the possible cause of its present decline. Certainly, to bring this coat to exhibition standard requires skill and time, but as a companion, where such perfection is not required, the coat should not be more demanding than that of any other long-coated breed. Probably the best known of the terrier breeds up to the end of the nineteenth century, the Skye can have either prick or drop ears, and

Sealyham Terrier

Skye Terrier

may be blue or fawn, with black points, in colour. Its height is 10 in., and its weight is 20 lb.

The Staffordshire Bull Terrier was not recognized until the 1930s by the English Kennel Club. In the U.S.A. it has been known since about 1870. A member of the bull terrier family, the Staffordshire seems to have a bit more bulldog and a bit less terrier in its makeup. Coming from the Black Country of Midland England, where it was bred from bull- and bear-baiting stock for the sport of dog fighting, the Staffordshire is strong and courageous. The Americans favour a heavier type and also crop the ears. Colours can be any brindle, black, blue, red, fawn, and white, or any of these with white. Its height is 16 in., and its weight is 38 lb.

Staffordshire Bull Terrier

The Welsh Terrier, intermediate in size between the Airedale and Lakeland Terriers, is an active sporting black-and-
tan dog. The ancestor of this and many of the other larger
terriers was the Broken-haired Black and Tan Terrier, which
was extinct as such by the beginning of the twentieth
century. The breed is a very sporting one and the dogs make
active and intelligent companions. The coat is hard, very
close and wiry. Colours are black and tan or black, grizzle
and tan. Its height is about 15 in., and its weight is about
20 lb.

The West Highland White Terrier is sturdy in build,
hardy in constitution and gay in temperament. It is a very
attractive offshoot of the Cairn family. Originating as 'sports'
in litters of normally coloured Cairns, these all-white terriers

Welsh Terrier

West Highland White Terrier

with the jaunty air have become more and more popular. They need very little trimming, and dirt brushes easily out of their short, hard coats. The body is well muscled with a relatively strong, thick tail. The dog's height is 11 in., and its weight is 18 lb.

The Soft-coated Wheaten Terrier, another terrier breed from Ireland, was recognized by the Kennel Club in Britain in 1943, but has not made much progress in England. The Wheaten Terrier has an abundant, soft, curly coat which must be of a good, clear wheaten colour. Puppies are born a red shade, with black tips to the hair, and this gradually lightens to the approved shade. In Ireland the dogs are required to have a working certificate before they can become champions. They are loyal and sporting terriers, unspoilt in any way. The dog's height is 17 in., and its weight is 35 lb. It is unknown in the U.S.A.

NON-SPORTING BREEDS

The utility group

The breeds in the Utility group have little in common with each other, ranging as they do from the fantastically popular Poodle to the little known Tibetan breeds.

The Boston Terrier was created by a group of men in and around Boston, Massachusetts, about 1870. They wanted a game fighting dog, and used the Bulldog and terriers in its creation. The markings and the round head which are so

Boston Terrier

Bulldog

distinctive of the breed were originally incidentals of the foundation stock. Recognized by the American Kennel Club in 1893, by 1903 it was the most popular dog in the United States, and remained so for the next twenty-five years. The dog's ears are cropped in its native land. The Boston did not become known in Britain until about 1935. The position of the white markings on the brindle is very important. The dog's weight is 15–25 lb.

The Bulldog has a scowling expression and a massive head that belie its gentle and affectionate nature. The modern

Bulldog bears little relation to anything that was pitted against a bull in the past. Now the nose is so short that the dog has difficulty in breathing, the jaw is so undershot that the grip is weakened, and the dog is too heavily built to be active. Its weight is 50–55 lb.

The Chow Chow is an ancient Chinese breed with a number of distinctive peculiarities. Its tongue is black and its hocks are straight. It is suspicious and aloof, and strictly a one-man dog. In their long history in their native land, Chow Chows are recorded as being used in many differing ways, from

Dalmatian

Chow Chow

hauling sledges in the north to acting as setters when hunting pheasant and *francolins* (a kind of partridge). The Chow Chow is also well-known in China for the delicacy of its flesh, having been bred for both meat and fur. Its minimum height is 18 in.

The Dalmatian was first imported into Britain in the eighteenth century, possibly from Dalmatia, on the western coast of Yugoslavia. Originally used as mail coach guards and carriage dogs, and being built to trot many miles after a horse, they like plenty of exercise. The spots can be either

125

black or liver and do not appear until the puppy is between two and three months old. The dog's height is 23 in., and its weight is 55 lb.

The French Bulldog was first imported into Britain in 1894, and it aroused considerable controversy because of its bat ears and its foreface, which does not have the typical Bulldog lay-back. However, English breeders had failed to produce a sound miniature Bulldog, so the French version stayed and to a certain extent prospered in Britain and the United States. The dog is a delightful character, sweet-tempered and affectionate, and not requiring too much in the way of either exercise or grooming. Its weight is up to 28 lb.

Hairless Dogs. Probably the most curious dogs in existence are the hairless varieties. All these breeds are rather terrier-like in appearance and very rare. They are believed to have originated in Africa, and been carried from there along the main trade routes of the world to the Americas and Asia. It is not known whether the hairlessness arose through a mutation or a malfunction of the hormone controlling hair growth, but it appears to be a dominant feature genetically. There are two sizes of MEXICAN HAIRLESS DOG, the larger of which is known in Britain. Weighing up to 36 lb., it is com-

French Bulldog

Mexican Hairless

parable in build to a Manchester Terrier. There is short, fairly coarse hair on the skull and the end of the tail. The skin can be mottled, bronze, elephant-grey, or black. The CHINESE CRESTED DOG is a small, pinscher-like animal with a long mop of hair, from which it gets its name, on its skull. The AFRICAN HAIRLESS DOG is unknown in Britain. All the hairless dogs are regarded as lively and affectionate in character. They are sensitive to cold and damp, and have a temperature several degrees higher than that of normal dogs.

The Keeshond is a Dutch breed that takes its name from a Dutch politician and reformer, Kees (Cornelis) de Gijselaar (1751–1815). De Gijselaar kept one of the breed, which became a symbol of the spirit of his people. Earlier, this type of dog had been widely kept as a guard on the Dutch barges. The defeat of de Gijselaar's patriots meant the eclipse of their symbol, the Keeshond, whose popularity did not really revive until the twentieth century. The breed has been exhibited in England for the last 40 years. The colour should be wolf to ash-grey, and the height is 18 in.

The Poodle is now one of the most popular of breeds, and from the number of references to it in art and literature it has always made influential friends. There are now three

Keeshond

recognized varieties, differing only in size. The oldest is the Standard Poodle, which must be over 15 inches in height. The Miniature Poodle was recognized in 1911 and has to be over 11 inches and under 15 inches. The Toy variety is smaller still, being under 11 inches in Britain, and under 10 inches in the United States. The Poodle originated in continental Europe, and is related to the water spaniels. It was known in Italy in the sixteenth century and in Holland in the seventeenth century, but did not arrive in Britain until considerably later. It was a sporting dog, used especially for retrieving from water, hence its name which derives from the German 'puddeln', to splash in water. This led owners to clip its hindquarters, so that the heavy coat would not impede swimming. The Poodle has always been noted for its intelligence, and has been used a great deal in circuses and performing acts. Poodles can be any solid colour. The profuse, offstanding coat is of hard texture and is usually clipped in the traditional 'lion' style.

The Schipperke (pronounced 'skipperkee' – it means 'little captain') is to Belgium what the Keeshond is to the Netherlands – a small, adaptable watchdog, bred for guarding canal

Standard, Miniature and Toy Poodles

Schipperke

boats. It was not until 1885, when the Queen of the Belgians became interested in it that it made any substantial headway in popularity. By 1890 a club had already been formed in Britain. Its foxy head and complete lack of tail give it a very distinctive outline. Although short, its coat is dense and abundant, with a mane and frill round the neck and 'culottes' on the back of the thighs. Its tail is docked very close and it is usually black in colour. It is both hardy and full of pep. Its height is 13 in., and its weight is 16 lb.

The Schnauzer is a German breed whose type was certainly fixed by the early seventeenth century. A statue of the Nightwatchman and his Dog in Stuttgart, dated 1620, shows a typical Schnauzer of medium size. The Giant Schnauzer, though widely used in Germany for police work and recognized in the United States, is practically unknown outside its native land. The Standard Schnauzer may be regarded as the breed prototype. Looking like a robust and squarely-built terrier, the Schnauzer is a general purpose working dog, reliable in temperament and with none of the terrier's aggressiveness or excitability. Standard Schnauzers and Miniatures both have harsh, wiry coats with prominent moustache and whiskers. The usual colours are either pepper

Shih Tzu

and salt or pure black. The standard height is 19 in., and miniatures should be under 14 in. Miniature Schnauzers are classified as terriers in the U.S.A.

The Shih Tzu (pronounced 'sheed-zoo') is one of a number of short-nosed breeds all originating in the Far East. It is related to the Tibetan Apso and is alert, arrogant, and courageous for its size. The number of people owning the dogs is growing steadily. The very long and profuse hair is coarser than that of a Pekinese, and falls forward over the eyes, while the plumed tail is carried over the back. The dog looks more massive than it is because of the wealth of coat.

Lhasa Apso

All colours are permissible, but a white blaze on the forehead and a white tip to the tail are prized. The dog's height is about 11 in., and its weight about 16 lb.

The Tibetan Apso, or Lhasa Apso, is possibly one of the ancestors of the Shih Tzu, to which it is very similar. Intelligent and hardy, the Apso makes a good watch dog. Like all the other Tibetan breeds, the Apso has a profuse coat and carries its tail gaily. Its height is 11 in.

The Tibetan Spaniel has a silky and profuse coat, with a distinct mane on the neck and shoulders. The top coat is flat and close but not particularly long, so that, compared with a Pekinese, to which it is similar in many respects, the Tibetan Spaniel appears high on the leg. It is supposed to have been bred in Tibetan monasteries. There, the smaller the dog was, the more it was prized. Its height is 11 in., and its weight is 16 lb.

The Tibetan Terrier resembles a larger version of the Tibetan Apso and is better known than the Tibetan Spaniel. The breed standard describes it as not unlike a miniature Old English Sheepdog. It is watchful, game and alert in character. There are only a few of the breed in Britain. Its height is up to 15 in., and its weight is up to 30 lb.

Tibetan Terrier

The working group

The working group contains the sheepdogs, cattle dogs, and guard dogs. Among these breeds are some used for police work and for guiding the blind. Intelligent and anxious to please, some of these dogs can become unreliable if wrongly handled or if their minds and bodies are under-exercised. However, they are also among the most rewarding dogs to keep because of their loyalty and willingness. Most of the giants of the dog world are in this group, and the cost of

Alaskan Malamute

Alsatian or German Shepherd Dog

feeding such dogs should always be taken into consideration before buying one.

The Alaskan Malamute belonged to one of the Innuit tribes in Alaska, and early explorers and missionaries praised the animal's endurance, fortitude and memory. Valued by their owners, Malamutes were treated better than most Arctic sledge dogs, and their fame was such that they were used by several modern Arctic expeditions. The Malamute is a strong, compact, muscular dog. Its thick double coat is either wolf-grey or black and white. Its face markings are a distinctive feature, either resembling a cap or a mask. Its height is 25 in., and its weight is 85 lb.

The Alsatian, or German Shepherd Dog, is the breed most widely used the world over for the exacting duties of police work and for guiding the blind. The breed was evolved in Germany. Originally a sheepdog, it is very unlikely that the Alsatian has any wolf blood, despite some superficial resemblances. They would not be used so widely by police and army were their temperament not reliable. All colours are allowed, but whites are not favoured. Its height is 26 in.

Karabash (Anatolian) Dog

The Karabash (Anatolian) Dog has recently been imported into Britain and recognized as a distinct breed by the English Kennel Club. It is probably a member of the mastiff group. There are several regional types in Turkey, where they are valued highly by shepherds as guards against wolves. Its coat is medium-short and dense, fawn or striped brindle with a black mask, ears, and tail. Its height is 29 in., and its weight is 124 lb.

The Australian Cattle Dog is recognized only in its country of origin. This breed resembles a miniature Alsatian and was created comparatively recently from blue-merle working

Bearded Collie

collies with a little Kelpie and Dingo blood. These dogs are used only for cattle droving and work silently. The short, harsh, weather-resisting coat is either red or blue speckled. Its head is long and fairly narrow, its back is short, its ears set high and erect, its legs are fairly long with compact feet. Its tail is long and carried low, though horizontal when excited. Its height is about 20 in.

The Bearded Collie was rescued from extinction after World War II. An old Scottish droving dog, the Beardie is a member of that ancient race of shaggy sheepdogs that are found right across Europe, and include the French Briard, the Hungarian Puli, and the Old English Sheepdog. Faithful and sagacious, the Bearded Collie is becoming slowly more popular. Colours are slate or reddish-fawn, which are preferred, but black, all shades of grey, brown and sandy are possible, with or without white markings. The coat is double – the under soft and close, the outer hard, strong and shaggy with a definite 'beard' on the muzzle. Its height is 22 in., and it is not yet recognized in the U.S.A.

The Bernese Mountain Dog is one of the most popular breeds in Switzerland, and is making headway in North America. It was originally a draught dog used by the basket

Bernese Mountain Dog

Border Collie

weavers of the Canton of Berne to take wagons loaded with
baskets to the market. A handsome, long-haired dog, the
Bernese is black and tan, with a snowy white chest. White
feet, a white tail tip, and a white blaze on the head are highly
prized. Its height is $27\frac{1}{2}$ in.

The Border Collie is pre-eminent among several strains of
working animals in Britain that certainly breed true to type,
but are not recognized as pedigree breeds by the Kennel
Club. They are however, recognized in Australia. The
Border Collies are the dogs that actually work sheep today,
as opposed to the show breeds of collie that once worked
but can do so no longer. Border Collie is perhaps a misnomer,
for though these collies may have originated in the Border
country of Scotland, they have been crossed freely with
Welsh and Cumberland sheepdogs with the sole purpose of
improving the working ability of the offspring. Lithe, brainy
dogs of immense stamina, they are usually black and white
or black, tan and white. Their working ability is so famed
that they have been exported to nearly every part of the
world where sheep are raised (often accompanied by a tape-
recording of the commands they are used to). They are
frequently used by obedience and working trial enthusiasts,

and compete favourably with Alsatians. The dog's height is up to $19\frac{1}{2}$ in., and its weight is up to 52 lb.

The Bouvier des Flandres is a cattle droving dog from south-western Flanders and northern France. It was formerly bred solely for work, and it was not until the 1920s that the breed became standardized. It has a docked tail, a harsh, tousled coat, and a pronounced beard. The dog's rugged strength and intelligence led to its use as an ambulance dog and a messenger dog in World War I. A Bouvier in Belgium cannot win the title of champion unless it has qualified in working trials. Its height is $27\frac{1}{2}$ in., and its weight is 77–88 lb. This breed is not classified in Britain.

The Boxer originated in Germany in the 1890s, and was created from the types of dog formerly used for bull-baiting. It first appeared in Britain before World War I. A strong, active, clean-cut animal, the Boxer is of the right size and temperament to be used for police work, as it is in Germany. The breed is cropped in some countries. Its height is 24 in., and its weight is 66 lb.

The Briard is a sheepdog now found commonly in all parts of France. It originated in the province of Brie, and records of this breed go back to the twelfth century. It is a strong, substantially-built dog, whose first duty was to protect

Boxer

Bouvier des Flandres

136

Briard

sheep against attacks by wolves. Now it is used as a guard and police dog, as well as for herding sheep. In build, the Briard is square, with a harsh, shaggy coat like a goat. In France, the Briard's ears are cropped enough to make them stand semi-erect, but in the United States they are usually left uncropped. Any solid colour is acceptable, the darker the better. Its height is 27 in. It is rare in Britain.

The Buhund is a Norwegian member of the Spitz family, and a utility farm dog in its own country. Fairly small, compact, and intelligent, the Buhund makes a good guard and companion. Though black is acceptable, most of those imported into Britain have been cream, wheaten, or light red. Its height is about 17 in. The breed is uncommon in Britain and unknown in America.

The Bullmastiff is pre-eminently a guard dog. It was created as such by crossing Bulldogs and Mastiffs, the former to give courage and pace, the latter to give size and weight. The type of animal produced was used by gamekeepers to protect their preserves against poachers, and became known as the 'Keeper's Night Dog'. By 1927, it was sufficiently distinct to be recognized by the Kennel Club in Britain as a breed. It is a one-man dog, prepared to defend its master's property to the utmost, and rather unwilling to share its master's affection with others. Its height is 27 in., and its weight is 130 lb.

Bullmastiff

Buhund

Rough Collie

Dobermann Pinscher

Smooth Collie

The Rough Collie, with its handsome long coat, has been consistently popular for many years on both sides of the Atlantic. Indigenous to Scotland, it has been refined by selective breeding, gaining in beauty of appearance while losing in working ability. Nowadays kept mainly as a companion for its looks and docility of temperament, the Rough Collie can be any colour, a showily-marked dog being preferred. Its height is 24 in., and its weight is 65 lb.

The Smooth-coated Collie is a more uncommon dog which should be an exact replica of the Rough except in coat. The Smooth is believed to have been a cattle dog originally in the North of England, and should have a short, harsh, weather-resisting double coat, often blue-merle in colour.

The Dobermann Pinscher is another breed produced in Germany, probably with the Rottweiler as part of the foundation stock. Supremely elegant in outline and aristocratic in bearing, it can be black, brown, or blue with tan markings. It is used as a guard dog and police dog in many countries. Its height is 26 in., and its weight is 75 lb.

The Great Dane is an ancient breed, a large, powerful dog of the proportions and type of the present Great Dane, having been known in Europe since pre-Christian times. Used for

Great Dane

Groenendael

boar hunting, the original Great Dane was heavier in build, resembling more closely the mastiff family to which it belongs. Now impressive in size and elegant in outline, the Great Dane is usually docile in temperament when properly treated. Its ears are cropped in some countries. It is an ideal companion and guard for those who can afford to feed and exercise a dog whose minimum height is 30 in., and minimum weight is 120 lb.

The Groenendael (pronounced 'groan-en-dale') – known in the United States as the Belgian Sheepdog – is one of the three kinds of sheepdog known in Belgium, which differ only in coat and colour. The Groenendael has a long-haired black coat and looks rather like a shaggy, black Alsatian. It is noted for its intelligence and working ability. Its height is 23 in., and its weight is 54 lb.

The Husky originated in Greenland, and should not be confused with the Siberian Husky, which is recognized as a separate breed by the American Kennel Club. The Greenland Husky, acknowledged as a breed in Britain, has a long, harsh outer coat which can be any colour, and the typical pricked

Husky

Komondor

ears and curled tail of the Spitz breeds. Of immense stamina, it needs plenty of exercise. Its height is 25 in., and its weight is 90 lb.

The Kelpie is Australia's native purebred sheepdog. The breed has erect ears, a pointed muzzle, and a short harsh coat which can be black and tan, blue and tan or red and tan. Whole colours are also permitted. The height is about nineteen inches and the weight 30 lb.

The Komondor (plural Komondorok) is the largest and probably the oldest of the Hungarian sheep and cattle dogs. It is believed to have come with the great Magyar migration from Asia. A large, powerful dog, needing plenty of exercise, it carries an enormous woolly, white coat. On the plains of Hungary this coat becomes completely matted or corded, protecting the dog from weather and enemies. Its height is 26 in. Classified by American Kennel Club only.

The Kuvasz is another Hungarian guard dog. The name suggests that it was brought to Hungary from Turkey or even farther east, probably by the Kurds in the twelfth century. In Hungary it became a dog of the aristocracy, being used as a hunter of big game and as a personal bodyguard. The present-day dog is 26 in. high at the shoulder, and weighing some 70 lb. Classified by American Kennel Club but not in Britain.

The Lurcher is not recognized as a pure breed, though the name has been in use since medieval times in Britain. A working dog of the gypsy and the poacher, the Lurcher is usually built like a greyhound for speed and has a short, wiry coat. For obvious reasons, dark-coloured dogs are preferred. Only a few strains of Lurcher breed true, as the name really covers all cross-bred Greyhounds and Whippets. Sheepdogs, Deerhounds, Retrievers, Salukis – all have been used to give the Greyhound cross the extra nose and stamina needed by a dog that is kept to catch meat for the pot. It seems likely that the Lurcher will soon be a dog of the past. Its height is about 26 in., and its weight is about 60–70 lb.

The Maremma is a popular sheepdog in central Italy though few are found elsewhere. With a long, lustrous white coat and a well-feathered tail, it is a handsome and tractable dog. Its height is 26 in., and its weight is about 75 lb.

Lurcher

Kuvasz

Maremma

The Mastiff was found in Britain by the invading Romans, who were so impressed by its ferocity and courage that they appointed a Procurator of Dogs in Britain to send Mastiffs to Rome to provide entertainment in the Roman arenas. Through the centuries it has been used as bull-, bear- and lion-baiting dog, as well as a guard. Unfortunately the very size of the animal has almost proved its undoing, as after World War II there were only a handful left in Britain. A few breeders mounted a rescue operation and now the dogs' numbers are such that their survival is assured. The Mastiff's minimum height is 30 in., and it should be as massive as possible.

The Newfoundland is one of the breeds famed for life-saving and is a relative of the St. Bernard, but exactly how it came to be in Newfoundland is not known. It was used in Newfoundland as a draught dog, for carrying burdens, and for hauling heavy fishing nets. Faithful and intelligent, the Newfoundland is a powerful swimmer, credited with a number of rescues of drowning people. Its colour is dull black, and its coat is flat, of medium length, coarse, slightly oily and capable of resisting water. Its height is 28 in., and

Newfoundland

Mastiff

its weight is 150 lb.

The Old English Sheepdog is a droving breed which possibly originated in the West of England. The profuse coat needs a good deal of grooming to prevent it from matting, but this is the only thing which can be said against the breed, members of which are sensible and devoted companions. The ambling walk is deceptive, as the dog is both agile and active. The minimum height is 22 in., but most animals of this breed are 25 in. or so.

The Puli (plural Pulik) is another Hungarian breed recognized in the United States. It is a medium-sized dog, used as a drover in Hungary, and valued as a house dog and companion elsewhere. The similarity to the Tibetan Terrier may be a clue to the breed's origin. The colour and texture of the coat is unique in the canine world. The black of the Puli's coat is dull and weatherworn, sometimes bronzed or sometimes greying, but always lacking in intensity. This black is typical, but whole grey or white Pulik are not unknown. In the adult, the woolly undercoat tangles with the top coat in such a manner as to form long cords. The first British Puli was shown in 1950. Its height is 17 in.

Old English Sheepdog

Puli

The Pyrenean Mountain Dog has been the shepherd's companion and the guardian of his flocks against wolves for centuries. It was taken to the French court in the seventeenth century, and became a pet of the nobility and the guardian of their chateaux. It is a close relative of the Kuvasz and the Maremma. In Britain it is probably amongst the most widely-kept of the very large breeds. Undoubtedly its magnificent white coat as well as its sweet-tempered character has a lot to do with this. Its height is up to 32 in., and its weight is 125 lb. It is known in the U.S. as the Great Pyrenees.

The Rottweiler (pronounced 'rot-vile-er') was developed in Germany around the market town of Rottweil. Supposedly descended from the cattle dogs with which the Romans used to herd the animals necessary to feed their invading armies, the breed remained a working dog for the cattle merchants of Württemberg. As more and more beef animals were transported by rail and the van replaced the draught dog, the Rottweiler became rarer. However, it was found to excel in police and army work, and this led to its revival. Its colour is black with well-defined mahogany markings. Its head is broad with a good stop and its tail is docked very short. Its height should be 25–27 in., and its build is substantial.

The St Bernard. The romantic story of the rescue of travellers lost in the snow of the Swiss Alps has meant that the St Bernard is one of the best-known breeds of dog, even if it is not one of the most widely kept. The monks of the Hospice of St Bernard have employed the breed's nose and sense of direction to find lost travellers for at least three centuries, and probably for much longer. 'Barry', a St Bernard now in Berne Museum, saved forty lives before losing its own. The smooth-coated variety is the older, the rough coat having been introduced with a Newfoundland cross in the early nineteenth century. The breed flourished in the late Victorian era. Its colours are orange, mahogany, brindle, red brindle, or white with patches of these colours. The dog's minimum height is $27\frac{1}{2}$ in.

The Samoyed was bred by the Samoyede people, who inhabit the tundras of northern Russia and Siberia, from the White Sea to the Yenisey river. A nomadic people, the Samoyedes used their dogs to guard their reindeer herds

Pyrenean Mountain Dog or Great Pyrenees

St. Bernard

Rottweiler

Samoyed

against wolves, to pull sledges, and to carry burdens. Like many northern races of dog, the Samoyed has a foxy head, pricked ears, a curly tail, and a close, dense, stand-off coat. It was first imported into Britain in 1889, and in 1909 the Club was founded. A happy and affectionate dog, it makes a good companion, and its white coat is harsh enough in texture not to pick up very much dirt. It has a soft undercoat. Its height is 21 in., and its weight is 55 lb.

Shetland Sheepdog

The Shetland Sheepdog has the charm of anything miniature. The modern trend is for smaller breeds to become the
most popular, so this tiny version of a Rough Collie would
seem assured of a bright future. The dog came originally
from the Shetland Islands, where not only the ponies
but also the cattle and sheep are on a small scale. In the
Zetland dialect they were known as 'peerie' or fairy dogs.
The first specimens were rather nondescript, but the breed
now has all the virtues of the large Rough Collie. Its outer
coat is long, harsh and straight with a soft undercoat. It has
a definite mane and its tail is long with abundant hair. Its
height is 14 in.

Belgian Tervuren

Cardigan Corgi

Pembroke Corgi

The Tervuren is a variety of Belgian Sheepdog unknown in Britain, but recognized by the American Kennel Club. The Tervuren has a coat that is a blackened-fawn in colour. The colour is of supreme importance, being the major difference between the Tervuren and the Groenendael. The dog's height is 26 in.

The Welsh Corgi has two varieties recognized as such by the Kennel Club in Britain since 1934. Of the two, the Pembrokeshire Corgi has far outstripped the Cardiganshire variety in popularity, to which Royal patronage has certainly contributed. Both dogs did the same work, as drover's dogs and farmyard guards. Built long and low so that they could rush in and nip the heels of the cattle without getting caught by the flying hooves, they still retain the loud bark, and sometimes the tendency to nip ankles, that made their ancestors so useful. Being short-legged meant also that they were used to work waterwheels and churn butter in the same way as turnspits did.

The Cardiganshire Corgi is the somewhat heavier of the two and has a long tail, resembling a fox's brush. Its colour is variable but never pure white and not predominantly red, like that of the Pembrokeshire Corgi. The Pembrokeshire Corgi has a docked tail, and makes an excellent house dog. Its colours are self red, sable, fawn, black and tan or with white markings on head, legs, chest and neck. The Corgi's height is 12 in., and the weight is 26 lb., for the Cardigan and 24 lb., for the Pembroke.

Australian Silky Terrier

The toy group

The toy group consists of nearly all the diminutive breeds developed solely to befriend and amuse mankind. Most toy breeds have long histories, and though the dogs are small in stature they often have big personalities and are completely fearless. Treated sensibly, they are not so delicate as many people seem to think. But as they have small litters, sometimes with difficulty, the prices of puppies can be quite high.

The Affenpinscher is known in the United States but unknown in Britain. It is a very old German breed which has rather been supplanted in favour by one of its descendants, the Brussels Griffon. Never still or quiet, but hardy and easy to manage, it makes an excellent companion. The Affenpinscher's apple head has bushy eyebrows and a moustache which, together with the docked tail, give it a monkey-like appearance – hence its nickname 'Monkey Dog'. White or light colours are undesirable. Its coat is stiff and wiry, and its ears are usually cropped. Its maximum height is $10\frac{1}{4}$ in., and the maximum weight is 10 lb.

The Australian Silky Terrier is also known as the Sydney Silky, in honour of its city of origin. Created mainly from Yorkshire and Australian Terriers, with a dash of Skye Terrier thrown in, the Silky has been regarded as a distinct breed in Australia for more than twenty-five years, and was recognized by the American Kennel Club in 1959. It is also recognized in India, where it is gaining in popularity. It first attracted attention in Britain about 1930. It is an agile, energetic toy terrier with intelligence and courage. Its coat is a silky blue and tan, and about six inches long, and it often has a dark mask. The tail is docked very close. Its height is 10 in., and its weight is 10 lb.

The Chihuahua (pronounced 'chi-wah-wah') originated in Mexico, and is believed to have been sacred to the Aztec people. The noble families are said to have often kept over a thousand dogs each with its attendant slave. Stone carvings show the dogs to have been known in Central America since the ninth century A.D. The modern Chihuahua is much smaller and comes in a much wider variety of colours than the Mexican original. They are alert, hardy little dogs with large, upstanding ears which add to the impression of intelligence. The fat, furry tail is of medium length and carried up over the back. Although so small and dainty all Chihuahuas should have a brisk, forceful action. Provided it is typical in shape, the smaller it is the better, the maximum weight being 6 lb. The smooth-coated and long-coated dogs are two separate varieties.

Affenpinscher

Chihuahua

The English Toy Terrier is the modern name for what used to be called a Black-and-Tan or Toy Manchester Terrier. Like its larger relation the Manchester Terrier, the English Toy Terrier was very popular in the 1870s, when the fashionable weight never exceeded 7 lb, but it has never been really fashionable since. Despite being so small these little dogs are true terriers and full of courage, and have been known to kill rats as large as themselves. It is black in colour, with bright tan markings, the placing and the shade of which are very important in a show specimen. It should have the true terrier gameness. The dog's maximum weight is 8 lb.

The Brussels Griffon first made its appearance in Belgium a little over a century ago. Developed from a rough-haired ratting dog, the Griffon's monkey face and impudent character assured it of many admirers. Spirited and active, the rough Griffon has a harsh, wiry coat and a definite beard. Colours are red, black or black and tan. The Brabançon is a smooth Griffon. The dog's weight is up to 9 lb.

The Italian Greyhound is believed to have existed for the past two thousand years. Italian Greyhounds are so delicate and graceful that they have been court favourites in all the capitals of Europe, and have been commemorated by appearing in portraits with their illustrious owners. It has been in Britain from at least the Tudor and Stuart periods. The dog's

English Toy Terrier or Toy Manchester Terrier

Italian Greyhound

Brussels Griffon

action should be like that of a hackney horse, and its coat as fine as satin. It is one of the few breeds that needs protection against the cold. Its height is 10 in., and its weight is 8 lb.

The King Charles Spaniel was named after King Charles II, who was extremely fond of his toy spaniels, most of which were of the black-and-tan variety. However, toy Spaniels or Comforters were known in Tudor times, and are believed to have come originally from Spain. There are four colour varieties of these little Spaniels – the black and tan or King Charles proper; the Tricolour or Prince Charles; the Ruby (a self-coloured rich, ruby red); and the Blenheim, a white dog with chestnut-red patches. The King Charles Spaniel is popular in the United States under the name of the English Toy Spaniel. The dog's weight is up to 14 lb.

The Cavalier King Charles Spaniel. At Cruft's in 1926, a New Yorker offered a prize of £25 for a dog most resembling the old-fashioned toy Spaniel as painted by Landseer. Interest was so great that two years later the Cavalier King Charles Spaniel Club was formed. This little dog has been popular ever since, though it is not yet recognized in the United States. They are however extremely popular since they are active, sporting and intelligent. There are four varieties, as with the King Charles, but the skull and muzzle shape are different. Its weight is up to 18 lb.

King Charles Spaniel or English Toy Spaniel

Cavalier King Charles Spaniel

Japanese Spaniel

Maltese Terrier

The Japanese Spaniel is a short-faced toy dog of Asian origin. Distantly related to the Pug and Pekinese, it has the dignity of bearing of the latter, while being higher on the leg and more sprightly in appearance. Originally it was considered delicate, which is one of the reasons why the hardier Pekinese overtook it in popularity. Its profuse straight coat is usually black and white. Its height is 10 in., and its weight is 4–9 lb.

The Maltese has a well documented history, going back to the pre-Christian era. It is believed to have come originally from Malta, and has been popular in the Mediterranean for many centuries. Though any self-colour is permitted, nearly all Maltese are distinguished by their long, white coats. The dog should not be over 10 in. in height or 10 lb. in weight.

The Miniature Pinscher is a breed manufactured by German dog breeders from a smooth-coated, medium-sized ratting dog. The breed became established in Britain after World

Papillon

Miniature Pinscher

War II. The dog's appearance is neat and stylish, from the small erect ears to the short, docked tail. It is lively, game and an alert watchdog. The colours should be red, black, or brown with tan markings. The height is 10 to 12 in.

The Papillon (pronounced 'pap-i-yon') is a member of the toy Spaniel family. The name refers to its large, upstanding ears, carried obliquely, which suggest the half-opened wings of a butterfly (French *papillon*). Of Franco-Belgian origin, it has long been a court favourite whose type has remained constant since it appeared in portraits painted by Peter Paul Rubens (1577–1640). The white blaze on the face, representing the body of the butterfly, should be well defined. The breed is popular in France and Belgium and was granted recognition in Britain in 1923. The dog's height is up to 11 in., and its weight is up to 7 lb.

The Pekinese should have heavy bone and a sturdy, well-built body. This may partly explain the toughness of both

Pug

Pekinese

body and character which have made the Pekinese the most popular toy dog of this century. Five were brought back from the looting of the Summer Palace in Peking in 1860, and one of these, 'Looty', was presented to Queen Victoria. From these and a few smuggled from China at the turn of the century all the dogs in the West are descended. After the death of the Empress Tzu Hsi in 1911, the fine Palace specimens became rare, and the breed has fallen into neglect in China. Profuseness of coat is matched by independence of spirit. The dog's weight should be 7–12 lb.

The Pomeranian is a dwarf version of a much larger, white Spitz-type dog, found extensively in northern Germany. Queen Victoria patronized the breed in 1888 and the Pomeranian became very popular in the early 1900s. In a surprisingly short space of time the white Spitz, weighing 25 lb., or more, had in fact given rise to a race of toys weighing about 5 lb., and being any of twelve recognized colour combinations. The Pomeranian's popularity waned somewhat as a result of competition from the Pekinese. It is a very active and vivacious little dog.

Pomeranian

Yorkshire Terrier

The Pug, a compact dog, is another short-nosed breed believed to have originated in China. Dutch traders took it home from Asia, and it reached Britain with the court of William III and Mary II in the late 1600s. The earliest Pugs were fawn, and the first black one was not shown until 1886. Its short coat is particularly free from doggy smell, and requires the minimum of care. It is rather larger and more robust than some of the other toy breeds. Colours are silver-fawn, apricot-fawn or black, with a black mask and ears in the first two. The dog's weight is 14–18 lb.

The Yorkshire Terrier was evolved by the working men in the weaving towns of northern England round about the 1850s. The first specimens were larger than those seen today, but length, colour and texture of coat were even then of paramount importance. The coat of an exhibition specimen is almost a full-time occupation for the terrier's owner, but underneath the hair there is a game little dog with a sensible, unexaggerated shape. The smallest are the most prized, but the larger ones with less coat make better pets. The dog's height is up to 8 in., and its weight up to 7 lb.

BOOKS TO READ

For general introductions to the subject the following titles are recommended and are usually available from bookshops and public libraries.

The Choice and Training of the Family Dog by John Holmes. Popular Dogs, London.

Dogs of the World by Dr. Erich Schneider-Leyer. Popular Dogs, London.

Man Meets Dog by Konrad Z. Lorenz. Methuen and Co. Ltd., London.

Champion Dogs of the World by Sir Richard Glyn. George G. Harrap and Co. Ltd., London.

The Complete Dog Book, the official publication of the American Kennel Club.

Know Your (breed). National Pet Library Inc., New York.

Dog Obedience Training by Milo Pearsall and Charles G. Leedham. Charles Scribner's Sons, New York.

The New Knowledge of Dog Behavior by Clarence Pfaffenberger. Howell Book House Inc., New York.

MAGAZINES

Our Dogs, Oxford Road Station Approach, Manchester 1.

Dog World, Press House, Wotton Road, Ashford, Kent.

Pure-Bred Dogs, American Kennel Gazette, 51, Madison Ave., New York. U.S.A.

Australian Dog World, Seadog Productions Pty. Ltd., Woollahra, N.S.W. Australia.

Kennel Review, L. Swales & Co., Mosman, N.S.W. Australia.

National Dog Newspaper, Daily Mirror, Sydney, N.S.W. Australia.

R.A.S. Kennel Control Journal, Paddington, N.S.W. Australia.

KENNEL CLUB ADDRESSES:

The Kennel Club, 1, Clarges Street, London, W.1.

American Kennel Club, 51, Madison Avenue, New York, N.Y. 10010, U.S.A.

The Australian National Kennel Council, Royal Showgrounds, Ascot Vale, Melbourne 3032, Australia.

INDEX

SOME OTHER TITLES IN THIS SERIES

Arts
Antique Furniture/Architecture/Art Nouveau for Collectors/Clocks
and Watches/Glass for Collectors/Jewellery/Musical Instruments/
Porcelain/Pottery/Silver for Collectors/Victoriana

Domestic Animals and Pets
Budgerigars/Cats/Dog Care/Dogs/Horses and Ponies/Pet Birds/Pets
for Children/Tropical Freshwater Aquaria/Tropical Marine Aquaria

Domestic Science
Flower Arranging

Gardening
Chrysanthemums/Garden Flowers/Garden Shrubs/House Plants/
Plants for Small Gardens/Roses

General Information
Aircraft/Arms and Armour/Coins and Medals/Espionage/Flags/
Fortune Telling/Freshwater Fishing/Guns/Military Uniforms/Motor
Boats and Boating/National Costumes of the world/Orders and
Decorations/Rockets and Missiles/Sailing/Sailing Ships and Sailing
Craft/Sea Fishing/Trains/Veteran and Vintage Cars/Warships

History and Mythology
Age of Shakespeare/Archaeology/Discovery of: Africa/The American
West/Australia/Japan/North America/South America/Great Land
Battles/Great Naval Battles/Myths and Legends of: Africa/Ancient
Egypt/Ancient Greece/Ancient Rome/India/The South Seas/
Witchcraft and Black Magic

Natural History
The Animal Kingdom/Animals of Australia and New Zealand/
Animals of Southern Asia/Bird Behaviour/Birds of Prey/Butterflies/
Evolution of Life/Fishes of the world/Fossil Man/A Guide to the
Seashore/Life in the Sea/Mammals of the world/Monkeys and
Apes/Natural History Collecting/The Plant Kingdom/Prehistoric
Animals/Seabirds/Seashells/Snakes of the world/Trees of the
world/Tropical Birds/Wild Cats

Popular Science
Astronomy/Atomic Energy/Chemistry/Computers at Work/The
Earth/Electricity/Electronics/Exploring the Planets/Heredity/
The Human Body/Mathematics/Microscopes and Microscopic Life/
Physics/Psychology/Undersea Exploration/The Weather Guide